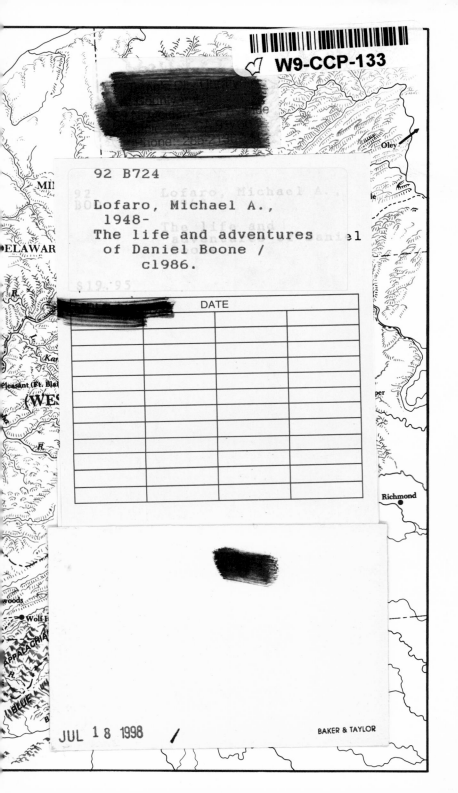

The Life
and Adventures of
DANIEL BOONE

Daniel Boone

The Life and Adventures of
DANIEL BOONE

MICHAEL A. LOFARO

THE UNIVERSITY PRESS OF KENTUCKY

Frontispiece:
Daniel Boone, painted in 1820 by Chester Harding.
Courtesy of the Massachusetts Historical Society, Boston.

The Life and Adventures of Daniel Boone was originally
published as part of the Kentucky Bicentennial Bookshelf.

Scholarly publisher for the Commonwealth,
serving Bellarmine College, Berea College, Centre
College of Kentucky, Eastern Kentucky University,
The Filson Club, Georgetown College, Kentucky
Historical Society, Kentucky State University,
Morehead State University, Murray State University,
Northern Kentucky University, Transylvania University,
University of Kentucky, University of Louisville,
and Western Kentucky University.

Editorial and Sales Offices: Lexington, Kentucky 40506-0024

Library of Congress Cataloging in Publication Data

Lofaro, Michael A., 1948–
    The life and adventures of Daniel Boone.

    Bibliography: p.
    Includes index.
    1. Boone, Daniel, 1734-1820. 2. Pioneers—Kentucky—
Biography. 3. Frontier and pioneer life—Kentucky.
4. Kentucky—Biography. I. Title.
F454.B66L63   1986   976.9'02'0924 [B]   85-31513
ISBN 0-8131-1593-0

Contents

Again,
for Nancy

Preface

THE EXISTENCE of a changing frontier has always exerted a great influence upon the American people. But from the time of Captain John Smith to the present day perhaps no one figure has been more central to the frontier experience than Daniel Boone. He is commonly regarded as the prototype and epitome of the American frontiersman.

Historically, nearly seventy of his eighty-six years were involved with the exploration and settlement of the frontier. In 1734 he was born on the western perimeter of civilization in Berks County, Pennsylvania. At the age of thirty-one he ventured as far south as Pensacola, Florida, in search of a new home. And when he died in 1820 he was living on the western boundary of civilization in St. Charles County, Missouri, one of the outposts for fitting out expeditions to explore the Rocky Mountains. Boone seemed constantly to place himself upon the cutting edge of civilization's advance.

Implicit in Boone is the typical inner conflict between civilization and the wilderness. He is both the pioneer who paves the way for civilized life and the natural man who prefers the simplicity and rugged vitality of a wilderness environment as an end in itself. To Boone, the frontier is simultaneously a challenge and an inspiration, something to subdue and improve and something to preserve and enjoy.

Boone's relationship to the wilderness accurately reflects a basic American attitude toward the frontier. For Americans, a frontier is not a boundary which indicates territorial limits but rather an area that invites and even demands exploration. There is a real and continuing desire to penetrate the unknown which has motivated American discoverers to take the first walk into the forests surrounding Jamestown in the seventeenth century as well as the first walk on the moon, the zenith of exploration of the "New Frontier" of the twentieth century. Daniel Boone's life is permeated by this same spirit.

Unfortunately Boone's relationship to his own historical period—the significant events in his life and their consequent bearing upon the development of America—is often a blur in the popular mind. Chronologically few place him as Washington's contemporary or the one who encouraged Abraham Lincoln, the grandfather of the sixteenth president, to move to Kentucky. Fewer still remember that the march of civilization into the trans-Appalachian West and beyond, areas opened by Boone and his fellow "Long Hunters," also brought with it the legal mechanisms used so dexterously to strip Boone of the nearly 100,000 acres of land he had acquired under what he thought was just claim. And yet he was never long defeated or discouraged. If the lawyers took his land or if the settlers who followed the trails he had blazed ruined the hunting, there was always more land and better hunting to be found further west.

In examining the life of Daniel Boone, it quickly becomes evident that he is the continual victim of a restlessness that occurs whenever the population around him grows too dense. As his uneasiness with civilization increases, he remedies the situation by plunging further into the wilderness. But in so doing he blazes a trail for others to follow. His example and fame unintentionally encourage rapid settlement, which only renews his restless spirit and forces him to move deeper into the forest. This outline of the general progression of events in Boone's life is far too simplistic to reflect accurately the total picture of his motives for exploration. It does show, however, the historical pattern that serves as the basis for the ambivalent attitude toward the frontier which marks Boone's image in biographies from 1784 to the present day, and perhaps provides the reader with an overview of the ironic cycle that at times seems to have dominated the frontiersman's life.

Boone has not been well served by most biographers. John Filson's "The Adventures of Col. *Daniel Boon* . . ." was published in 1784 as part of his *The Discovery, Settlement And present State of Kentucke*. It was the first printed account of Boone's life. Unfortunately Filson's bombastic, ghost-written retelling of the pioneer's "autobiographical" adventures represented the frontiersman as more a philosopher than an Indian fighter and contained a number of historical inaccuracies. Yet the information gleaned from Filson's personal interviews with Boone and his companions still managed to shine through the rhetoric. Since the "Adventures" consisted of Boone's life from 1769 to 1782 and chronicled one of the most vibrant and exciting eras in American history, a number of quotations from Filson's Boone are incorporated in the sections of this book that deal with this period. The statements are usually described as coming from the "autobiography" to warn the reader that in all likelihood these are not Boone's actual phrases.

In general, these fourteen years are well documented in regard to Boone. His boyhood and to a lesser extent his later years, however, are times for which the scope of events may never be known fully. Twice the aged Boone attempted to dictate his life's story to a relative, and twice the resulting manuscript was lost. Such disasters, of course, only enhance the value of Filson's work. But his narrative is neither the sole nor the main source of material for this biography. For a more complete description, please see the "Bibliographic Note" at the end of the volume.

A major problem in writing a biography of a figure whose name evokes almost instantaneous initial recognition and then subsequent confusion as to dates, events, and places (other than Kentucky), is the matter of tone and approach. It is perhaps as impossible as it is undesirable to write a biography of Daniel Boone that does not tend in some ways toward the romantic. His life is simply suffused with drama and color, the stuff romance is made of. In trying to give an accurate, orderly exposition of the actual occurrences in the pioneer's life, I attempt to stress the distinction between legend and popular belief on the one hand and documented fact on the other. In Boone's case, myth and man can be separated to their mutual advantage. Stories, tales, and events that persistently crop up in his life, but whose authenticity or degree of truth cannot be verified, are labeled as traditional materials.

I should like to express my sincere appreciation to all those who have offered assistance and encouragement in the preparation of this volume. These include Ms. Katherine Bartlett of the Museum of Northern Arizona; Mr. John D. Cushing of the Massachusetts Historical Society; Dr. Thomas Field of the Department of Geography at the University of Kentucky; Dr. F. Gerald Ham and Dr. Josephine L. Harper of the State Historical Society of Wisconsin; Mrs. Eugenia Y. Jacobs of the Washington County Historical Society, Washington, Pennsylvania; Ms. Lou Delle McIntosh of the Department of Parks, Frankfort, Kentucky; and Ms. Lucy Ude of the Washington University Gallery of Art, St. Louis, Missouri. I extend my special thanks to Mr. Nelson L. Dawson, the editor of *The Filson Club Historical Quarterly*, for his continuing help with my Boone projects, and to the Filson Club of Louisville, Kentucky, for its willingness to share its many unique resources and materials.

My colleagues and friends, particularly Drs. Richard Beale Davis, John Hurt Fisher, James C. Klotter, and Martin P. Rice, and Mr. Howell P. Boone and Mr. Louis R. Boone, have given me words of advice and cheer at times when they were most welcome. I am grateful for a grant from the Better English Fund, established by Dr. John C. Hodges for the Department of English of the University of Tennessee, which supported the travel and research expenses necessary to complete this book. Ms. Carolyn F. Goodwin's excellent typing has made the preparation of the manuscript a far easier task.

Both my parents, Mr. and Mrs. Anthony L. Lofaro, and my wife's, Mr. and Mrs. Stephen J. Durish, have provided the aid and understanding that only parents can supply. And finally, I thank my wife Nancy for her insightful comments, keen-eyed proofreading, and indexing. Without her dedicated help, the writing of this biography would have been neither possible nor pleasurable.

1

THE EARLY YEARS

DANIEL BOONE was a supremely active man who seemed to come by his zest for adventure quite naturally. On August 17, 1717, his grandfather George Boone took the courageous step of uprooting his large family from the sleepy village of Bradninch in England and sailing to America. A weaver by trade, George Boone was fifty-one years of age and well past the time when one would normally determine to start a new life. But he was driven by two motives, the same two motives which later directed the actions of his famous grandson: he wanted freedom and he wanted land.

George Boone was a dissenter, a Quaker. He had heard remarkable tales of a sanctuary for Quakers in the New World, a colony founded by William Penn, where no one was persecuted for religious beliefs. Sects such as the Quakers, Mennonites, and Dunkers, the German Baptist Brethren, lived together in peaceful coexistence with the Indians. And cheap land was available in the 28-million-acre land grant that came to be known as Pennsylvania. All this news must have seemed an answer to George Boone's prayers. Yet he was not an impetuous man. He refused to base a remove across the Atlantic upon rumor and supposition; he demanded direct knowledge and facts. Sometime before 1713, probably in 1712, he sent three of his children—George, Sarah, and Squire—to investigate the land of promise. Squire, the future father of the famous woodsman, shipped out as a cabin boy.

The land they explored and the prospects they anticipated impressed the threesome quite favorably. Sarah and Squire remained in America and George returned to Devonshire with a glowing report. His father, however, delayed four years more before committing himself, his wife Mary, and their children to the rigors of the voyage and resettlement. The younger George returned immediately and was wed by May 1713. Eventually the Boones did embark on their journey, traveling eighty miles by land to Bristol, where they took passage for America. By October 10, 1717, they landed in Philadelphia, a small but growing city.

The Boones first settled some twelve to fourteen miles north of Philadelphia in Abington (now Montgomery County) in a community composed nearly exclusively of Friends. But they soon moved on. As John Bakeless, Boone's definitive biographer, aptly put it: "They did not stay. There was always a branch of the Boone family that never stayed. The Boones were wanderers born. They had the itching foot. Something called. Something beyond the mountains always whispered. They heard of distant lands and knew that they must go there."

They first transplanted themselves only a few miles away to the village of North Wales in Gwynedd Township. George Boone was accepted into the Gwynedd Meeting after producing "a Certificate of his Good Life from the Monthly att Callumpton In Great Britain." His daughter Sarah married Jacob Stover and settled in Oley Township (now Berks County), a setting which so pleased George Boone that on one of his visits in 1718 he took out a warrant for 400 acres of land. He is believed to have moved the family to Oley within two years.

On July 23, 1720, Squire Boone married Sarah Morgan, a descendant of the early Welsh inhabitants of Gwynedd. Squire followed both his father's trade as a weaver and his father's propensity for acquiring land. His industry and frugality allowed him to purchase 147 acres in New Britain Township in Bucks County on December 3, 1728. At the close of 1730 he obtained 250 more acres from one Ralph Asheton. He, Sarah, and their four children moved to this site in Oley, which adjoined his father's land, sometime early in 1731.

2

On this Berks County farm on November 2, 1734, a sixth child was born to Squire and Sarah Boone. He was called Daniel. His parents may have named him for a distinguished Dutch painter, Daniel Boone, who died in London in 1698 and was perhaps a distant relative. If Daniel was indeed named for this artist, the boy, although truly appreciative of nature's beauties, exhibited little inclination toward passive endeavors such as painting.

The story of his early youth, which survives for the most part in legend and anecdote, is nevertheless a keenly attuned preview of his future exploits. He loved his freedom and was irked by anything that restrained it. He easily forgot his duties as the family's herdsman and wandered delightedly in a wilderness yet unchanged by civilization. He was a hunter, a fighter, a stout comrade. And he was a boy. He possessed a boy's sense of humor and commanded some respect as an adept prankster. Young Daniel was all this and much more. He and his family sensed that he was different, somehow unsuited to the more domestic aspects of their lifestyle. He helped with the farm, learned rudimentary blacksmithing, and perhaps helped his father in the family trade of weaving. Still, his constant obsession was the chase. Only when hunting or trapping did he seem to feel truly and fully alive.

The earliest information about young Daniel concerns a smallpox epidemic which broke out in Oley when he was a small boy. To prevent her children from exposure to the dread disease, Mrs. Boone confined them at home. Little Daniel and his next older sister, Elizabeth, soon concluded, with the irrefutable logic of children, that the way to eliminate the restrictions under which they suffered was to contract the disease, for once over it they could resume their normal activities. The decision reached, they sneaked out of bed one evening, stole away to a neighbor's farm, and lay down beside a victim of the disease, probably one of their stricken playmates. Then they triumphantly made their way home and crept back into their beds undiscovered, gleefully awaiting the red blotches that would be the harbingers of their freedom. Mrs. Boone all too soon recognized the symptoms which she

3

had vigorously tried to prevent, and riveting her eyes upon Daniel, calmly asked him to tell her "the whole truth." He made a full confession of his simple solution to his problem. Too concerned to chide him overmuch, she told him how badly he had behaved and fretfully added: "Why did thee not tell me before so that I could have had thee better prepared?" Daniel, as did Elizabeth and the other Boone children, recovered with no complications. He regained his cherished freedom of movement. The pox had been a great success.

In October 1744, Squire Boone purchased twenty-five acres of grazing land in Oley some five or six miles north of his homestead. From the age of ten until he was sixteen Daniel regularly accompanied his mother, who always took charge of the dairy, on the annual migration to the site. They lived during the grazing season, from spring to late fall, in a small rustic cabin built under some shady trees by a swift-flowing brook. Daniel's job as herdsman tantalized him with many opportunities to neglect the cattle. Often he would slip away into the woods for days at a time. One of his relatives remarked that Daniel was "ever unpracticed in the business of farming, but grew up a woodsman & a hunter." His only weapon was what he called his "herdsman's club," a staff so shaved from a small sapling as to create a lethal point from the rooty knob at its end. During his nomadic wanderings Daniel became expert in killing small game with a single toss of the spearlike club. When Daniel was twelve or thirteen his father yielded to his pleas and presented him with a short-barreled rifle. Daniel was overjoyed. He took it upon himself to keep the family larder filled with fresh game. He became a crack shot for his age and began to take extended winter journeys to the Flying Hills and the Oley Hills, to the west and north of the Monockasy Valley, and to the Neversink Mountains. He was never to stop his explorations; he would continue to range further and further in his hunts to the south and west.

Daniel Boone's formal education is a much disputed matter. He insisted to his children that he never went to school a day in his life. His older brother Samuel's wife, Sarah Day, is said to have taught him the rudiments of the three Rs, but a glance at any of his letters reveals that he never completely mastered spelling and grammar. One legend has it that his uncle John Boone, a schoolteacher, gave up trying to improve Daniel's composition as a lost cause. Squire Boone was said to have responded to John's despair with the now famous remark, "Let the girls do the spelling and Dan will do the shooting." No worse a grammarian than many a frontier hero such as Simon Kenton and George Rogers Clark, Daniel was, however, the only "creative" speller of George Boone's forty-five surviving grandchildren.

On the other side of the question of education, a whimsical tale survives that concerns the tiny country school which Daniel supposedly attended. The teacher was a dissipated Irishman whose mood fluctuated violently. He would grow despondent with his charges, excuse himself from the room, and return minutes later with a much brightened countenance to deliver an enlivened, animated lecture. One day when chasing a squirrel in the woods nearby, Daniel stumbled upon the source of his teacher's inspiration—a bottle of whiskey hidden in the underbrush. After a quick conference, Daniel and the older boys hit upon what they thought would be a just compensation for the Irishman's too free application of the hickory switch; they mixed a potent tartar emetic with the whiskey. Needless to say, the next journey out to the thicket resulted in the return of a less than cheerful instructor, whose usually reddened face was blanched and strained. He called upon Daniel to solve a mathematical problem. Young Boone blurted out the wrong answer and was whipped with heavy strokes for his error. The blows kept coming. The other children screamed and shouted. The somewhat bewildered Daniel knocked the teacher down and ran for the woods. The Irishman, not Daniel, was dismissed. Boone was said never again to have ventured into any formal institution of learning. Nature became his sole teacher, experience and observation his guides.

Like most boys, Daniel Boone had a special friend. Henry Miller, two or three years Daniel's senior, worked in Squire Boone's smithy repairing guns and farm implements. Daniel, as his pupil, became competent at metal work, at least as it related to the rifle. Boone and Miller were a congenial, lively pair who were unduly fond of mischief. Any farmer they thought offensive might well find his wagon disassembled and its wheels handsomely displayed on his barn roof or dangling from a treetop.

The prankish duo once learned that George Wilcoxen, a neighbor of Squire Boone who was entirely unfamiliar with firearms, wished to borrow a long musket to try his hand at deer hunting. He requested that Squire load the gun for him so it would be ready for early morning use. Unnoticed, the boys took the gun, withdrew the ball, and added six additional charges of powder. The ball was reloaded and the musket secretly replaced. Wilcoxen set out at sunrise, no doubt reciting to himself the various instructions given him by his friends. Boone and Miller had begun to doubt the wisdom of their deed; they knew the overloaded musket might burst and seriously injure the unsuspecting hunter. Their thoughts were interrupted by a noise that sounded like the report of a small cannon. They ran forward and, much to their relief, met Wilcoxen returning. His face was bruised and bloodied from a gash in his forehead. The kick of that "darned gun," he said, had knocked him to the ground. Squire Boone saw Wilcoxen and earnestly inquired how all this mayhem came about. When Wilcoxen related the story and laid the blame for his wounds to the musket, Squire Boone vigorously protested that the load was so light he could have rested the breech of the gun on his nose and fired it without the least danger. The boys interrupted to ask Wilcoxen if he had killed a deer. He replied that he had a fair shot, but was so affected by the force of the ensuing blast that he did not notice if he had hit the animal. He added wryly, however, that he thought it was a pretty *dear* shot. Daniel and Henry found the dead deer and brought it in for the novice woodsman, who ever after loaded his musket himself.

Another of the boys' deeds did not escape misfortune. They had learned of a frolic in a distant settlement and decided to attend without asking Squire Boone's permission, for they knew that because of his Quaker beliefs he would categorically refuse. Hoping to make a grand entrance, they appropriated Squire Boone's best horse and set off double-mounted for an evening's entertainment. On their return they tried to jump the horse over one of Squire's old cows which lay quietly in the path to the stable. The cow bolted up just as the horse was in the midst of its leap. The horse fell with a sickening crunch; it had broken its neck. Daniel and Henry, bruised but uninjured, resolved to keep the incident secret. They put the saddle and bridle back in their proper places in the barn and crept stealthily into bed. Poor Squire never was able to figure out how a horse could break its own neck in an open field.

The Boones were not typical Quakers. They were peaceful people but ready to defend their possessions and rights with their lives. In 1728 when there was great fear of an Indian uprising, Daniel's grandfather George wrote to the governor that though the general populace had fled there remained "about twenty men with me to guard my mill, . . . and we are resolved to defend ourselves to the last Extremity." Young Daniel, although not pugnacious, was involved in a boy's normal share of disputes.

A very different incident, however, demonstrated that frontier gallantry, at least for Daniel, depended upon the actions of the fair sex. Once two needy neighbor girls, who were going to Mrs. Boone's to bring home the remainder of a plentiful catch of shad for their mother, emptied a pail of fish entrails upon the sleeping Daniel's face as a joke. They went home with the shad, bloodied noses, and swollen faces. Their mother soon presented herself to Mrs. Boone to demand that the young ruffian be punished. Sarah Boone, the most devout Quaker of the family, gave a reply that bristled with the Boone family spirit: "If thee has not brought up thy daughters to better behavior, it is high time they were taught good manners. And if Daniel has given them a lesson, I hope, for my part, that it will, in the end, do them no harm; and I have only to add, that I bid thee good day."

The records of the Exeter Quaker Meeting testify that the Boones were not always in accord with the doctrines of the

7

Friends. In 1742, Sarah, Daniel's oldest sister, married outside the order and subsequently was disowned by the Society when they discovered that she was with child before the wedding. Called to account, Squire Boone confessed "himself in a Fault" in regard to his daughter's unapproved marriage, but stated "that he was in a great streight in not knowing what to do, seeing he was somewhat Sensible that they had been too Conversant before." Five years later, Squire's son Israel married a non-Quaker, and although no scandal was involved, he too was disowned. On this occasion Squire expressed no contrition and in fact insisted on Israel's right to marry whomever he pleased. Still not recanting his position after a few months, Squire Boone was judged unfit for membership in the Meeting and was expelled.

Squire Boone was in a quandary. He had fallen from grace with the Society of Friends and forfeited his leading position in the Meeting. His businesses were doing well, but social pressures mounted to such a degree that he resolved to leave Berks County. The desire to see each of his children with good land, now too costly to obtain in Pennsylvania, and the rapidly decreasing fertility of his own fields due to current agricultural methods, undoubtedly contributed to the decision as well. A little more than two years after his expulsion, having disposed of all nonessentials, Squire Boone led his family out of Pennsylvania on May 1, 1750. Their destination was uncertain. His wife Sarah, still a Friend in good standing, requested and received letters attesting to her good character addressed to meetings in Virginia, Maryland, and North Carolina.

The little caravan wended its way west to Carlisle and then down the Cumberland Valley and into the Shenandoah Valley. The Boones tarried perhaps two years on Linnville Creek, a half dozen miles north of Harrisonburg, Virginia. Here, Henry Miller decided to leave the pioneer band and make his home near the residence of Squire's good friend from Berks County, John Lincoln, whose great-grandson would one day be the sixteenth president. Daniel did not see his friend again for thirty years. When they did meet, one was a well-to-do businessman and one a living legend of the American frontier.

8

Sometime between the fall of 1751 and the spring of 1752 the Boones reached the Yadkin Valley of North Carolina. In the present Davie County, Squire built his new home on Dutchman's Creek, a tributary of the Yadkin River, at a place called the Buffalo Lick. Late in 1753 he purchased 640 acres of choice land. Surrounded by a wilderness abundant in deer, turkey, otter, beaver, muskrat, and some buffalo, Daniel, nearly twenty years old, evinced even less interest in farming than he had as a boy in Pennsylvania. The Yadkin region was the extreme western frontier; it had very little of civilization about it. A mediocre hunter could bring down four or five deer in a day; Daniel Boone could kill thirty. Daniel helped the family by transporting pelts, furs, and produce to Salisbury during the summer, but took advantage of every opportunity to indulge the hunter's roving life.

By this time his extraordinary marksmanship was common knowledge. His ability with a rifle almost led to his first encounter with a hostile Indian. Daniel was an expert student of Indian habits and hunting techniques and he had known only the most amicable of relationships with his forest brethren. His sharpshooting, however, soon excited the jealousy of Saucy Jack, a Catawba warrior who felt his abilities with a gun were the equal of Boone's. Despondent that his claim was supported only by himself, Jack, after bolstering his courage with whiskey, announced his plan to kill his rival. Daniel was away hunting. When Squire Boone heard of the threat against his son, he could not control his wrath. He grabbed a hatchet and rushed out after Saucy Jack yelling that "if it has come to this, I'll kill first!" Someone luckily warned the Catawba, who fled toward his village some sixty miles distant. The Boones were not a family to be trifled with.

2

WAR, LOVE, AND
THE URGE TO RAMBLE

DANIEL BOONE would get his first taste of Indian warfare all too soon. England and France were both strongly pressing their claims to the Ohio Valley, part of which was later to become Kentucky. England asserted its right to the territory under the Virginia charter of 1609 and the explorations of Thomas Batts and Robert Fallam, who took possession of the region for the crown in 1671. They claimed English sovereignty over the lands drained by the New River and the lands associated with the waters into which that river emptied. By claiming the New River, a tributary of the Ohio, they were in effect claiming the entire Ohio Valley. France, which cited the exploration of the Ohio River by La Salle in 1669 as authority for its continued presence, had perhaps validated its title more effectively than England by establishing a series of sparsely settled frontier outposts from New Orleans to Canada. England had no permanent settlements to verify its contentions.

In practical terms France's close-knit alliances with the Indians increased its control of the Ohio region. The French had actively courted Indian support since the beginning of the eighteenth century with a good deal of success. Unlike the British, they accepted the Indians, intermarried, and did not consistently seek to displace them from their lands. The relatively few Frenchmen in the Ohio Valley—fur traders, Jesuit missionaries, and government officials—posed no immediate threat to the Indians' land since the areas they took for settlement, sometimes by force, were proportionally small. By comparison, between 1745 and 1754 the council of Virginia granted in excess of 2.5 million acres in the Ohio Valley to speculators.

The British colonies had no united policy in regard to the Indians and those colonies that emphasized trade, such as Virginia and Pennsylvania, competed for furs with each other as well as with the French. English influence was originally great among the Iroquois, Cherokees, and Shawnees in the seventeenth century but waned early in the eighteenth. The Iroquois were no longer a dominant force and the overlords of various tribes. The Shawnees were disillusioned when Pennsylvania recognized the Iroquois as the sole rightful claimant to the land drained by the Delaware River. The British also did not openly seek friendship with a race they thought barbaric in action and culture. The French evinced very different views and successfully wooed many tribes to their cause.

The 1748 treaty of Aix-la-Chapelle brought the outright hostilities of King George's War to a halt in the New World, but still left the struggle for control of the Ohio Valley unresolved. Major merchants in England urged the immediate resumption of the war to eliminate France as a commercial rival and their pleas were aggressively seconded by colonial leaders who hoped for large territorial gains. War was not declared. But the Greenbrier, Loyal, and Ohio companies made significant efforts to settle the Ohio region and concurrently, from 1748 to 1753, the French moved to consolidate their position with the Indians with shows of strength designed to intimidate and prevent trade with the English.

The border disputes between the French and their Indian allies and the British over control of the Ohio Valley escalated rapidly. The French had to keep the English settlers east of the Appalachian Mountains; they would brook no migration that would drive away the game upon which their immensely lucrative fur trade depended. Great Britain's position on the other hand, while also viewing America as a vast source of raw materials, was essentially that of the empire-building provider. The American colonies were a large market for English products, and the more immigrants, the larger the demand. But new immigrants needed land which the settled seaboard regions could no longer offer. The lines of battle had been drawn. The missions undertaken to demand French withdrawal from Fort Le Boeuf by a relatively unknown young colonial major of militia named George Washington in October 1753, and which climaxed in his bloody defeat by the French and Indians at Fort Necessity in July 1754, snuffed out the last flickering hope of peace. In effect, the French and Indian War had begun.

By April 1755, Major-General Edward Braddock had arrived in Virginia with two regiments of British regulars and taken charge of all British and colonial troops in America. He was an arrogant, overbearing bulldog of a soldier, and a master of European warfare. He informed Benjamin Franklin, who was helping to provide supplies and transportation for the army's baggage in Pennsylvania, that Fort Duquesne was an easy mark that would not detain him more than three or four days. Then he would push on to Niagara and, after securing that position, to Frontenac. Knowing Braddock's unfamiliarity with frontier fighting, Franklin warned the brash officer that the Indians were "dextrous in laying and executing ambuscades." Braddock retorted that "the Savages may be formidable to your raw American militia; upon the king's regulars and disciplined troops it is impossible they should make any impression."

Among Braddock's forces were men destined to affect each other's fate. Washington, now a colonel, was attached to Braddock's staff, and a British lieutenant-colonel named Gage commanded the advance guard. Twenty years later Gage would be besieged in Boston by the Virginian. And two lesser personages, Daniel Boone and John Findley (or Finley), had signed on as wagoners for the expedition. Findley, an Irish adventurer and Indian trader, had recently returned from the hunter's paradise—Kentucky. In Boone, his stories found an avid audience. From him Daniel learned of a way to get to Kentucky through the great gap in the Cumberland Mountains, and from there to follow the "Warriors' Path" to the Ohio River. These fireside tales of a fertile land where buffalo and deer were so plentiful that they were there just for the taking excited Boone's imagination and ambition beyond measure.

In retrospect, Boone's meeting with Findley was perhaps the one bright spot of Braddock's campaign. The general's blunders were legion. He had no conception of forest warfare and no intention of using the colonial militia, the only troops experienced in Indian fighting. He humiliated them by stationing them far to the rear in his column, saying they possessed "little courage or good will." The march from Virginia began on April 2. Boone and his baggage wagon trailed close behind the British artillery as they crawled toward Fort Duquesne for weeks. The historian George Bancroft commented that Braddock's army stopped "to level every molehill, and erect bridges over every creek" before proceeding. On July 9 the force finally passed the Monongahela River and got within seven miles of the fort "with colors flying, drums beating, and fifes playing the *Grenadiers' March.*"

Braddock's every move—his deployment of troops, reconnaissance, and bivouac—was a model military maneuver. The French were terrified and willing to surrender. Only a subordinate officer named De Beaujeu was valiant enough to rally a band of French soldiers, Canadians, and Indians to attack Gage's advance guard. The British were moving along a path through the forest but twelve feet wide and were ambushed as they entered Turtle Creek Ravine. Their enemies seemed to be behind every tree, bush, and rock; all were under cover. Gage's men, though they outnumbered the attackers, could not rout them. When the main column arrived, Braddock and his officers exerted every effort to form their failing ranks of regulars into lines in the open in the finest textbook tradition of European battle. The Indians marvelled at the magnificent targets their red coats made, and continued the slaughter.

Braddock was mortally wounded, De Beaujeu killed. Washington, rising from his sickbed, rallied the provincials to cover the retreat frontier-style. They followed the motto "every man to his own tree" and slowed but could not stop the rampaging Indian pursuit.

Boone and the other wagoners, who had been ordered not to retreat, watched the regulars flee by them to the rear. Realizing that to remain with a heavily laden wagon would be suicide, Boone vaulted onto his team, cut the traces, and galloped to safety. Findley and the other teamsters followed suit; they were the fortunate ones. The historian Draper noted that twelve regulars, fresh from Europe, surrendered to the Indians. They did not understand why they were stripped naked and painted black, nor did they comprehend their fate until the first soldier "was tied naked to a stake, with his hands fastened above his head, then tortured with red hot irons, and lighted pine splinters stuck in his body; and the shrieks of the victim, drowned in the horrid yells of his tormentors as they gaily danced around him, gradually became fainter and fainter." One after another, continued the previously captured James Smith, the prisoners were "burned to death on the banks of the Allegheny River opposite to the fort."

To his dying day, Boone condemned Braddock's decisions and methods. He was extremely critical of the lack of scouts and the failure to employ strong flank guards. Daniel made his way back to the Yadkin. For him, the results of the campaign were simple. He had his dream of Kentucky and his scalp.

In the settlement, Daniel renewed his acquaintance with a girl named Rebecca Bryan. He had first met her in the fall of 1753 when his sister Mary married Rebecca's brother William. Rebecca was now seventeen and Daniel twenty-one. She was above average in height, of dark complexion, and had jet black hair and eyes. He was described as "five feet eight inches in height, with broad chest and shoulders, his form gradually tapering downward to his extremities; his hair moderately black; blue eyes arched with yellowish eye-brows; his lips thin, with a mouth peculiarly wide; a countenance fair and ruddy, with a nose a little bordering on the Roman order."

They went cherry-picking with a group of young people, but managed to isolate themselves sufficiently to engage in a mild flirtation. Boone was taken with the beautiful girl and wondered what type of wife she would be. Feeling a little uncomfortable talking to Rebecca, Daniel drew his knife and began to slash absentmindedly at the grass around them. It may have been by accident or, as Boone ever after insisted, by design, but the wayward knife cut a large hole in Rebecca's white cambric apron, a rare article of finery on the frontier. He waited for her reaction, he said, for he chose this method "to try her temper." Rebecca neither wept, scolded, nor gave any indication that she was annoyed with the "accident." She was so pleasant about it that she may have seen through the entire scheme. In any case, Daniel had found his future wife.

Only two events of their courtship were recorded. One, a patently false story concerning the couple's first meeting which gained widespread belief, seems to have been concocted by Timothy Flint for his 1833 biography of Boone. According to the tale, Daniel was "fire-hunting" one night, sighted his prey, and raised his rifle to shoot the "deer" whose eyes reflected the torch's light. Some premonition stayed his trigger finger, and the deer, Rebecca, bounded home yelling that she was being chased by a panther. A variant of the tale has Boone killing the kitten Rebecca held in her arms when he "shined" its eyes. None of the Boone children ever believed the tale.

Daniel did, however, according to frontier custom, appear one day at his fiancée's door to demonstrate his skill in dressing out a deer which he had killed to indicate his ability as a provider. He launched lustily into his task, but was mocked by some of the young female onlookers because of the blood and grease that besmeared his hunting shirt. Daniel didn't say a word. When the young people later sat down to eat, Daniel picked up the bowl placed before him, studied it, and said: "You, like my hunting shirt, have missed many a good washing." The barb hit home. Rebecca's sisters were shocked at this comment on their housekeeping. Daniel had evened the score.

Daniel and Rebecca were married on August 14, 1756. After living for a while in a cabin in his father's yard, they moved a few miles north and settled on Sugar Tree Creek. Here they resided for ten years except during times of impending Indian invasion. Half of their children were born in this period: James (1757), Israel (1759), Susannah (1760), Jemima (1762), and Lavinia or Levina (1766). In the first two years of their married life Daniel farmed, worked occasionally as a wagoner, and made fall and winter hunts. The period from 1758 to 1760, however, saw the North Carolina border embroiled in a series of Indian wars brought on by the wanton murder of several Cherokees by whites. Some of the Boones and Bryans took refuge in Fort Dobbs. Old Squire Boone retreated to Maryland, and Daniel brought Rebecca and his two young sons, James and Israel, to Culpeper County, Virginia.

Boone may have enlisted as a wagon master in General John Forbes's 1758 expedition against Fort Duquesne. If the story Boone told to a friend many years later was true, it would confirm his participation in the campaign. Daniel said that he killed his first Indian by throwing the attacking brave off the Juniata bridge and onto the rocks far below. The only troops near the Juniata River at this time were those of Forbes.

While in Virginia, Daniel supported his family by hauling tobacco to the market at Fredericksburg. The only surviving anecdote connected with his stay in Culpeper County chronicles a portion of one such trip. Isaiah Boone, Daniel's nephew, stated that one of Boone's employers sent a black to give the wagoner a neck piece of bull beef for his provision. Boone, suspecting that the clammy meat could only be from one of Noah's cattle that had survived the many years since the Flood, told the slave to lay it down. The black put it on a stump and gazed dumbfoundedly as Boone seized a billet of wood and beat the bull beef all around the ground at a furious rate. His strokes kept the black dodging artfully from place to place to protect his shins. When done, Boone replied off-handedly to the black's question as to the reason for his curious action by saying: "I thought it looked plaguy tough and I was only trying to see if I could possibly make it tender; but it's all to no purpose." The slave reported the incident to his master, who took the rather broad hint and saw that Boone ever after dined as well as himself.

By October 12, 1759, Daniel had returned to the Yadkin. A purchase of 640 acres of land "from his father for 50 pounds" was recorded on that date. Although his family probably remained in Virginia, Daniel always appeared to be too restless to enjoy the farmer's or tradesman's life. During the temporary cessation of Indian hostilities, he plunged into his beloved wilderness and made his first journey across the Blue Ridge, penetrating as far as Boone's Creek in the present Washington County, East Tennessee. About a hundred miles from the Cherokee towns on the Little Tennessee River he carved the now famous 14- by 19-inch inscription: "D. Boon cilled [sic] a Bar on tree in the year 1760." The hunting was fine.

Passing through the Yadkin Valley on his return to Culpeper, Boone learned that a mopping up operation against the Cherokees was soon to take place. In Virginia he sold the fruits of his hunt, provided for his family, and was back in North Carolina by late summer to enlist under Colonel Hugh Waddell. By November 1760 the Cherokee nation had been broken. They had been badly beaten on all fronts and driven into hiding in the mountains. Their villages and crops had been burned. Surrender was inevitable. What contributions Boone made on this campaign are unknown. He was present, however, on November 19, 1760, for the signing of the peace treaty at Fort Robinson, a newly constructed outpost on the Long Island of the Holston River.

Daniel indulged in another hunt after Waddell's regiment disbanded. At the head of a group of Yadkin men he again roamed through East Tennessee and then into southwestern Virginia. One of his companions was Nathaniel Gist, the son of Christopher Gist, Washington's famous scout. Thoughts of Kentucky may have been reanimated in Boone's mind on this excursion. Nathaniel undoubtedly spoke of his father's explo-

17

rations in the land beyond the mountains and he and Daniel probably made Kentucky a main topic of campfire conversation.

The hunt was finished in the spring of 1761. Boone returned to his home on Sugar Tree Creek, put in and harvested a crop, and went to Culpeper to retrieve his family. They arrived at the Forks of the Yadkin sometime early in 1762. The next year in the life of the Boones was uneventful. The business at hand was setting the farm in order.

Not all frontier inhabitants resolutely began such work. The constant flights to the forts during the French and Indian War had bred a criminal element. To be able to reap a crop was so unlikely in those troubled times that many found it not worth the effort to sow. Even worse, they found an easy source of income through "appropriating" and selling the abandoned horses, cattle, tools, and furniture of the absent settlers. After the war the thieves continued to ply their trade. Groups of irate border citizens in the Carolinas banded together, calling themselves Regulators, and sought to bring immediate justice to the criminals. When horse-thieves and other desperadoes were caught, they were tried by a kangaroo court and, if found guilty, punished on the spot. The Regulators justified their actions on the grounds that some judges and sheriffs were in league with the bandits or easily bribed. Some officials practiced their own brand of thievery by charging exorbitant fees or taxes for marriage licenses, registering land claims, and other matters that required legal approval. The people were polarized, often along political lines. It was all too much for Daniel Boone. He tolerated no robbers, but took little interest in the machinations of political intrigue. He had a simple solution to governmental oppression—he could move beyond the reach of the government and its agents. But matters were not that bad, at least not yet.

At this time there was an organized group of a dozen thieves who were the scourge of the Yadkin country. Two of the outlaws even kidnapped the daughter of a neighboring farmer. Boone, stung by the audacity of the deed, headed one of the pursuing parties. They boldly pressed along the trail and came across the girl, who had escaped while her captors battled over the possession of their prize. Led back to the spot by the girl, they found one kidnapper disabled and bleeding profusely; the other had fled. The wounded brigand was jailed, but his eventual fate is not known.

Nearly a year later a cache of stolen goods was found under the fodder stack of a Yadkin man named Cornelius Howard. Confronted with the evidence, he confessed his connection with the bandits and agreed to lead a party to the thieves' mountain fortress. With Howard's help, Boone and his men surrounded the distant camp, rushed it, and captured several of the band, including a couple named Owens. Large quantities of stolen goods were recovered from the stockaded cave and various other hiding places in the surrounding area. Mrs. Owens, evidently feigning illness, asked to see Howard. When he appeared, he was nearly dispatched by the concealed pistol she drew. Frustrated when the gun was snatched from her hand, "she gave him a pretty fair specimen of low invective, branding him as a second Judas." The name stuck. All the captured criminals except "Judas" Howard were taken to the Salisbury jail to await trial. Howard, freed because of his cooperation in breaking up the gang, was ambushed and killed several years later as he was crossing a stream on his horse. The assassin was never apprehended.

Settlement was increasing on the Yadkin. Boone had to range further and further for game. On these long rambles he acquainted himself thoroughly with the beautiful mountains of western North Carolina. On his shorter trips, perhaps as early as 1764, he began to initiate his eldest son James in the ways of the woods. Sometimes the winter weather was so severe that Daniel could keep his little son warm only by buttoning him inside his buckskin hunting jacket as they lay before their campfire. As James grew up, he continued to accompany his father on the fall hunt and gave every indication of developing into a true frontiersman. No one, certainly, could impugn the credentials of his tutor.

In 1765 Daniel Boone had an unexpected run-in with an old hunter named Tate. Returning from one of his hunts, he learned that Tate, a man who hardly ever left the woods, had neglected to lay by enough food for his family. Since he planned to thresh out some rye for his own family's use on his father-in-law's land, Boone asked for and received permission to cut additional grain for Mrs. Tate. Tate returned, was outraged at Boone's action, which placed Tate in a poor light as a provider, and evidently began muttering around the settlement that Boone was paying too much attention to another man's wife. Daniel was furious. He beat Tate severely and threatened to do it again if Tate mouthed any more of these petty jealousies over an act of kindness for which anyone but a fool would be extremely grateful. The incident was closed, but it added a bit more encouragement for Boone to move on.

In the late summer of that year, a timely and unique opportunity presented itself at Boone's door in the person of Major John Field. Field, William Hill, a man named Slaughter, and two of Boone's other militia comrades from Culpeper County were off to explore Florida, recently ceded to Britain by Spain, with an eye toward the hundred acres of free land granted by the British government to each new Protestant immigrant. Daniel quickly accepted Field's invitation to join the group. The Yadkin was becoming far too civilized to suit his tastes and Florida might just prove to be the solution. His younger brother Squire, recently married, and their brother-in-law John Stuart also decided to try their luck to the south. Daniel bid Rebecca goodbye and promised to try to be home in time for Christmas dinner.

Five hundred taxing miles later they reached Florida and explored the eastern, central, and western portions of the colony. It was a place of contrasts. Strangely beautiful natural fountains and luxuriant flowers and foliage gladdened their view, but much of the country was wretched swampland, a nearly impassable quagmire. Along the many waterways the soil was rich, but two hundred yards inland it was too sandy to support a crop. On one leg of their journey they found so little game that they nearly starved to death. Stuart lost his way searching for food and stumbled back upon his companions days later in a pitiable state. When they encountered a camp of Seminole Indians, Squire Boone fortuitously gave an Indian girl a small shaving-glass. The gift, which delighted the young girl, allayed the suspicions of the Indians and gained an abundant store of venison and honey for the woebegone travelers.

Despite the paucity of game and inestimable numbers of alligators, bullfrogs, and stinging insects of the inland areas, the coastal regions, especially the bay at Pensacola, pleased Daniel. On the spur of the moment he bought a house and town lot and seemed intent upon making Florida his new home. The eight weary explorers turned toward Carolina and arrived four months after their August departure. Along the way, Slaughter, a competent gambler, won almost enough money in the towns they passed through to offset their total expenditures. If the few deerskins taken along the way were added in, the account books were even.

Daniel slowed his pace as he neared Sugar Tree Creek so that he strode into his cabin on the stroke of noon on December 25, giving his "little girl" Rebecca and his children their most hoped-for Christmas gift. Throughout a joyful dinner he described the hardships and privations of his Florida adventures. Imagine Rebecca's surprise when Daniel announced his purchase and his desire to relocate the family there. For the first time, and also the last insofar as history records, Rebecca flatly refused to accede to her husband's wishes. She saw nothing favorable about the place for her, the children, or Daniel. They would be too far from friends and relatives. Boone mulled over his spouse's comments and agreed. The house, lot, and migration to Florida were abandoned.

About this time Benjamin Cutbirth married a niece of Daniel Boone. Boone, a lover of solitude, found in Cutbirth one of his few compatible hunting companions. On one unsuccessful trip into East Tennessee, they were robbed of a large quantity of furs and skins and all their equipment by a party of Cherokees. They also hunted together for bears in Ashe County in the far northwestern corner of North Carolina. There Boone would often use any spare time to gather ginseng for market. For some reason Daniel did not accompany Cutbirth and three other Long Hunters on an astounding journey which began in the summer of 1767. They made their way through the wilds of Tennessee to the Mississippi River and spent one or two years in winter hunts and spring descents by river to sell their goods at New Orleans. They suffered badly at the hands of the Creek nation on their return to Carolina, however, and vowed never to make the trip again.

Meanwhile, in the autumn of 1767, Boone decided to explore Kentucky. After a dozen years he still remembered Findley's grand stories. With his brother Squire and William Hill, Daniel crossed the Blue Ridge and Allegheny mountains and the Holston and Clinch river valleys and reached the Big Sandy River. He believed the Sandy would lead them to the Ohio and would provide a natural entrance into Kentucky. They followed its banks for about a hundred miles on a journey which put them west of the Cumberland Mountains. Here they were "ketched in a snow storm" and elected to keep winter camp near a salt spring ten miles west of the present town of Prestonsburg, Kentucky. There was no want of fresh meat. Great numbers of buffalo and deer frequented the spring. Boone killed his first buffalo here. But as the winter weather mellowed, the journey west was hampered by increasingly rugged terrain. The forbidding hills, overrun with laurel, forced them to abandon their quest and trudge back to the Yadkin. Boone and the others did not realize that they had been in Kentucky. Only a few days' journey would have brought them to the fertile plains of bluegrass and cane which Findley had described.

3

KENTUCKY

DANIEL BOONE had now explored to the north, south, east, and west. He weighed the advantages and drawbacks of immigration in each general direction and determined that his new home would be to the west, to the land of greatest risk and greatest reward—to Kentucky. Boone and many other Americans who drew the same conclusion were, in effect, willing to disregard the British Proclamation of 1763, which forbade settlement west of the Alleghenies.

After conquering and winning the Ohio Valley, England intended, according to Lord Barrington, to maintain the region from the mountains to the Mississippi as "a desert for the Indians to hunt in and inhabit." Current English thought on the appropriate function of the colonies led in part to this Indian "preserve" theory. One commentator's remark was typical: "British colonies are to be regarded in no other light, but as subservient to the commerce of their mother country; the colonists are merely factors for the purpose of trade, and in all considerations concerning the colonies, this must always be the leading idea." The colonies were viewed essentially as a market for finished products, and the Indians as suppliers of needed raw materials. Any wholesale incursion into the Indians' hunting grounds would ignite a destructive war that would in turn disrupt the lucrative fur and Indian trade which occupied so much of the attention of the Board of Trade in London.

Similar commercial worries were also tinged with political ramifications. Practically speaking, the West and Canada were limitless areas whose remoteness from the Atlantic seaboard would place the aggressive settler beyond English mercantile control. The fear was that he might organize trading with the Indians which would limit the availability of cheap raw materials, or might even set up factories that would reduce the colonies' demand for British manufactured goods. Underlying all these apprehensions was the disturbing concept that immigration to the new territories would inevitably encourage colonial independence.

The Proclamation of 1763 was untenable at the time of its decree. The Carolinas, Virginia, Connecticut, and Pennsylvania all had charters which granted them land west of the Allegheny Mountains. The crown previously had no uniform Indian policy and had left negotiations and agreements up to each of the colonies. The resulting overlap in alliances and boundaries threw the actual ownership of various tracts of land into doubt and made the Indians suspicious of the whites' true intentions in the Ohio Valley. To many colonists it seemed that possession would determine legal title in this ambiguous situation. An additional incentive to settlement in the forbidden region was the growing discontent of people with their present lot. New outposts sprang up rapidly as they sought a better life in the West.

Daniel Boone was no exception to this trend. From 1766 to 1768, he moved westward three times. Game was scarce around Sugar Tree Creek and the increasing population was more and more oppressed by the extortions of court clerks, tax gatherers, sheriffs, and lawyers. One example of the frauds perpetrated concerned land agents who issued patents and later discovered that one of the many titles of the landholder (the Earl of Granville) had been "mistakenly" omitted. The patents had to be reissued and a second fee paid or the title would be declared worthless. To avoid such problems, Boone first moved sixty miles northwest toward the headwaters of the Yadkin, then five miles further upriver, where he erected another cabin about a half mile up Beaver Creek. He finally settled on the southern bank of the Upper Yadkin just above the mouth of Beaver Creek.

Daniel was pleased with his new situation. He had more game and less aggravation. He still sought the exhilaration of long hunts. One winter night, near the present city of Jonesborough in East Tennessee, he was aroused from a deep sleep when his snow-covered blanket was gently raised by an Indian. The warrior recognized Boone and delightedly exclaimed "Ah, Wide-Mouth, have I got you now?" Undaunted, Daniel got up and gave each of the band a hearty handshake and stated how happy he was to see his red brothers. After exchanging civilities, news, and comments on the hunting (Daniel undoubtedly knew a little of the Indian tongue and the Indians probably spoke some English), Boone was allowed to depart. He lost no time in putting a considerable distance between himself and his "brothers."

During the winter of 1768–1769 the Boones received an unexpected visitor. Over thirteen years had elapsed since Braddock's defeat, but somehow John Findley, now an itinerant peddler, had found his old comrade's rustic cabin. He had again descended the Ohio in 1767 and carried on a very successful fur trading business with the Indians. But one man in a canoe could bring out only so much in goods. He wished to return to that land of quick profit by an overland route but readily admitted he was no expert woodsman. Rivers or Indians had always been his guides. When he heard Daniel and Squire relate their failure to reach Kentucky by way of the Big Sandy, Findley explained, in more detail than he had years before, how the Warriors' Path, used by the Cherokees to attack the Shawnees and other northern Indian tribes, led through a gap in the Cumberland Mountains and into Kentucky. But Findley was unsure of how to find the Warriors' Path. He knew it was further west than the Boones had penetrated in 1767, but that was all. He needed a guide. Daniel did not have to be asked twice.

Findley's visit was a turning point in Boone's life. Daniel's "scratch" farming, never vigorously pursued, could barely provide for his family. He was being sued for nonpayment of debts at the court in Salisbury and consequently was mired deeper in debt by the legal fees he owed to Richard Henderson's law firm. Judge Henderson was himself interested in western land speculation on a grand scale. Apparently as early as 1764 Boone had been gathering information about the trans-Appalachian wilderness from hunters and trappers, stating that he was employed by Henderson and company to explore this region. But the land Henderson thought to gain through a royal grant was acknowledged as belonging to the Cherokees by the treaty signed in October 1768 at Hard Labor, South Carolina. This treaty, coupled with the ever-increasing white migration, made it imperative that Henderson negotiate directly with the Indians, and as quickly as possible. When Boone appeared in court in March 1769, he was accompanied by his brother-in-law John Stuart and by John Findley. Henderson was to defend Boone. Although no one can be sure, it is likely that the coincidence of Boone's desires and Henderson's needs made Kentucky a far more discussed topic than the lawsuit. Henderson, probably also at this meeting, agreed to finance an expedition.

Boone, Stuart, and Findley, together with three men— Joseph Holden, James Mooney, and William Cooley or Cool, who were employed as camp-keepers and common hunters—comprised the band of adventurers. All the men put in their corn crops and Squire remained behind to help all the families with the harvest. The six men left from Boone's cabin on the Upper Yadkin on May 1, 1769. They scaled the Blue Ridge, crossed the three forks of New River, and passed over Stone Mountain at a place called "The Stairs." They proceeded over Iron Mountain, across Holston Valley, through Moccasin Gap, and across the Clinch River, Powell's Mountain, and Walden's Ridge. Upon entering Powell's Valley, they found Joseph Martin's party erecting the then westernmost settlement of Martin's Station. In Powell's Valley they ran across a hunter's trail that led them through Cumberland Gap and to the Warriors' Path. They followed the path for many miles, crossed numerous creeks, and finally camped at Round Stone Lick Fork on the west branch of the Rockcastle River.

Daniel thought that the meadowlands of Kentucky could not be far from the camp and set off to climb the highest knob on the distant ridge separating the Rockcastle and Kentucky rivers. From its summit he saw his dream. He could see what is now Garrard and Madison counties, and beyond. Findley, meanwhile, had gone off in search of his previous trading site on Lulbegrud Creek. He had an easy task. The Warriors' Path, which ran along the west bank of a creek and crossed the Kentucky River, led straight to the Indian town of Eskippakithika on Lulbegrud. He returned about ten days later with his report. The adventurers soon crossed the ridge near the high knob which Boone had ascended, and by June 7 made their first base camp near the creek Findley had followed. Its name still bears testimony to their presence—Station Camp Creek.

Hunting was their immediate task. Deerskins were in prime condition in the summer and fall and were needed in quantity to repay the money probably advanced by Henderson. They brought forty cents a pound at market. Since the average skin weighed approximately two and one-half pounds, each was worth one dollar, or, in hunter's parlance, "one buck." The hunters worked in pairs. Boone and Stuart formed one team and Findley and one of the camp-keepers the other. The remaining camp-keepers had the job of preparing the skins for market and "jerking" enough meat for winter and spring supply. All went well. No matter how many excursions Boone made, he continued to marvel at the beauty around him. The "autobiography" recorded that even in winter he could say "Nature was here a series of wonders, and a fund of delight."

On December 22, Boone and Stuart went hunting, as they had done many times before. They had yet to see the first sign of Indians. But near the Kentucky River at the end of that day, they were surprised by a mounted party of Shawnee braves on their way home to Ohio from hunting on the Green River. Captain Will, their leader, demanded to be shown their camps. Uplifted tomahawks indicated the consequence of refusal. Daniel "cheerfully" agreed and set slowly about leading the Shawnees to each of their outcamps, where the plunder would be insignificant. At the first stop, Boone managed to

warn off the camp-keeper unnoticed by the Indians. He felt
sure that the man would head immediately to the main camp,
warn the others, and remove the accumulated skins of six
months' hunting.

To Daniel's amazement and dismay, when they ultimately
came to the main camp, nothing had been taken away. He
later remarked that truly "the time of our sorrow was now arrived." The Indians confiscated the skins, guns, ammunition,
horses, and every other article of worth. Captain Will, technically at peace with the English and well pleased with his good
fortune, equipped each captive with a small trading gun, some
powder and shot, a doeskin for patch leather, and two pairs of
moccasins. He then ordered his "brothers" to "go home and
stay there," explaining that "this is the Indians' hunting
ground, and all the animals, skins and furs are ours."

Findley and the camp-keepers, who were evidently too
frightened to take the time to hide their goods, soon reap-
peared. These four wanted to give up and go home. Boone,
however, persuaded them to stay near the camp while he and
Stuart attempted to raid the Indian band and retake at least
one or two horses. After two days they overtook the braves
during the night and stole four or five horses. A full day's and
night's hard ride later, they stopped to rest the animals. Stuart
bent down to tie his moccasin and, with his head near the
ground, thought he heard a rumbling noise. The next instant
the Shawnees thundered down upon them. They had discovered the theft early and had pursued the whites with their
fleetest horses. They laughed at the hunters' failure, tied a
horsebell around Boone's neck, and forced him to caper about
while they chided him by repeating "Steal horse, eh?"

The prisoners were told they would not be released until
they reached the Ohio. They passed the next seven days under
close surveillance and were bound at night. While the warriors
were making camp near the present town of Maysville, Kentucky, Boone and Stuart each grabbed a gun and bolted into a
thick cane patch, where they remained until the Indians gave
up the search. They retraced the seven days' trip in twenty-
four hours, only to find their camp abandoned. The others

28

thought they were dead. The dying embers of the campfire indicated a recent departure. The weary duo struggled on for thirty-five or forty miles before overtaking their companions on the Rockcastle River. Daniel was overjoyed to find his brother Squire, who, coming out to Kentucky with Alexander Neely, had met Findley and the retreating party. Squire's appearance with more horses, traps, and ammunition gave Boone an option which he chose to exercise. He would remain in the wilderness to hunt and trap rather than go back to Carolina in debt. Squire, Stuart, and Neely also resolved to stay, while Findley, Holden, Mooney, and Cooley chose to depart for civilization.

Having learned all too well the lesson of setting up camp too close to the Warriors' Path, Daniel made a camp on the northern bank of the Kentucky River not far from the mouth of the Red River and devoted himself to trapping beaver and otter. In top winter condition, beaver pelts were worth about two and one-half dollars each and otter pelts about three to five dollars. Thus winter trapping was the most lucrative of hunts. A horse normally could carry one hundred deerskins, or about 250 pounds, a load valued at one hundred dollars. A horse load of beaver pelts was worth five times as much. It was no wonder that they built a canoe to make their trapping more efficient.

Daniel and John Stuart continued as a team but, well acquainted with the country, agreed to divide their traps and meet at an assigned place about every two weeks. In late January or early February, Stuart took the canoe and crossed the Kentucky. Boone attributed his failure to return to the recently rain-swollen river. But Stuart never came back. When Boone could ford the river, he began a search. All he found was a cold campfire and the initials "J.S." freshly cut in a nearby tree. The mystery remained unsolved until five years later when one of Boone's axmen, who was helping to cut the Wilderness Road, found a man's bones in a hollow sycamore near the Rockcastle River crossing, miles from Stuart's former campsite. A powder horn was also found in the tree; engraved on the brass band encircling it were Stuart's initials. The discoloration produced by a leaden ball was visible at a break in the left arm, but no other injury could be discovered. Boone surmised that Stuart had been wounded by Indians and escaped, but in trying to get to a place to cross the river was forced to crawl into the tree for protection from the elements and died from loss of blood.

Daniel and Squire Boone were able to deal philosophically with their brother-in-law's disappearance. Men died in the wilderness. It was that simple. Neely's ability to cope was not the equal of the Boones' and he set off alone for home. The Boones erected a sturdier cabin, or "cottage," as Daniel called it, for the winter and kept busy trapping. Anxiety over the danger of Indian attack understandably was ever present but, according to Daniel, the fear was more than soothed by their beautiful surroundings: "Thus situated, many hundred miles from our families in the howling wilderness, I believe few would have equally enjoyed the happiness we experienced."

The winter and spring trapping was a great success, but their ammunition was nearly exhausted. They packed the pelts and on May 1, 1770, Squire returned home to market them, settle some of their debts, and get "a new recruit of horses and ammunition." Daniel was left alone, "without bread, salt or sugar, without company of any fellow creatures, or even a horse or dog." Why did he not accompany Squire? He missed his family, he did not have enough powder and shot to hunt commercially, and he could not trap this late in the season. Evidently he stayed to explore, to learn all he could about Kentucky for himself and probably for Richard Henderson.

Boone traveled throughout the Kentucky and Licking valleys and examined the Ohio as low as the Falls (present-day Louisville). Although the signs and sounds of Indians were all around him, he was not discovered. He made Indian-type camps and when ready to retire at night slipped off some distance from the dying fire and slept in the cane. At any hint of danger Daniel would head for a canebrake. The dense, entwined masses of cane stretched on for miles in places and grew ten, twenty, and sometimes even thirty feet high. It was next to impossible to track a man who took refuge there. Boone also visited the Upper and Lower Blue Licks and watched immense herds of buffalo come to lick the salty ground or drink the brackish water. He inspected the famous Big Bone Lick and was intrigued by the large quantity of fossil remains of mammoths. After exploring the Ohio and then reaching the Kentucky River near Leestown, just north of Frankfort, Boone observed an Indian fishing from a fallen tree which partially extended over the water. All he ever said of the incident was that "while I was looking at the fellow, he tumbled into the river, and I saw him no more." Daniel's tone and expression assured his family that he had been looking at the Indian over the sights of "Old Tick-Licker," his favorite rifle. Revenge? Self-defense? Boone never revealed his motives for the act.

He soon went further up the Kentucky River, camped in a large cave in Mercer County, and carved "D.B.—1770" on a nearby tree. While roaming along the high ridge of Dick's (now Dix) River, Daniel found himself hemmed in by Indians. He had two choices—surrender or jump. He jumped, landed where he had aimed, in the thick top of a small sugar maple on a second bank far below, quickly clambered down the tree, and stole off unseen beneath the overhanging boughs. The Indians peered over the cliff and knew that this must be a charmed white man. The bank was sixty feet down.

This was a time of adventure for Daniel and he enjoyed it to the utmost. The southern novelist William Gilmore Simms has perhaps best captured the romance of Boone's solitary stay: "His life was one of excitements, and a certain sense of insecurity heightened his enjoyment. He lived in sight of loveliness, but on the verge of danger. Beauty came to him, with Terror looking over her shoulder. . . . He pursues no old paths, but, reconnoitering the country, gathers a new horizon with every sunrise."

Boone continued his exploring until, as they had agreed, he met his brother at their old camp on July 27, 1770. Squire told Daniel that their families were well and had been provided for, that he had paid some debts and procured new supplies. They moved the camp a few miles down the Kentucky to another cave near the mouth of Hickman Creek. Once when

31

they returned to one of their outcamps, they thought that it had been ransacked by Indians. Moccasins, leggins, blankets, and even the camp kettle were gone. They soon saw wolf tracks. Following the trail, they found the full kettle licked clean and the blankets ripped in shreds, the better to line a den full of cubs. They killed the old thief, but could not train the cubs. Daniel said that despite his best efforts they were wolves still. He always seemed to have bad luck with wolves. Another raided the camp and made off with his hat. Boone hated coonskin caps and always insisted on a hat. He was not about to let this one get away and be without a replacement until he reached the settlements. A quick shot decided the matter. Daniel's "civilized" hat was back in its proper place.

The Boones had good hunting. In autumn Squire once more took the skins back to the Yadkin and purchased new supplies. Probably because of heavy rains, his return was delayed beyond the allotted time and Daniel set off to the east either to meet his brother or to continue on home rather than spend another season alone in the wilderness without proper provisions.

Along the way, he came upon an ancient Indian who had been left to die by his tribe. Pitying the old man's situation, Daniel retraced his steps a half mile to a deer he had just killed and brought the rest of the meat back to the helpless Indian, who manifested sincere gratitude for the kindness. Such concern seemed in direct contrast to his slaying of the Indian who was fishing, but typified the ambivalent attitude which existed in Indian-white relations at the time. A sense of kinship through the common activity of hunting could allow these men to see themselves as "brothers" in a certain sense. Why did Boone help the old Indian and in other much more equivocal circumstances show similar compassion? Why did Captain Will recapture Boone and Stuart rather than killing them outright for disobeying his commands? Perhaps as fellow woodsmen and hunters they did recognize and respect their mutual love for untamed nature. However, Boone and the other whites were speculators in land, or men whom speculators would follow. They were the harbingers of civilization before which the wilderness would retreat. Both sides knew or suspected that conflict was inevitable and both were capable of initiating what would logically appear to be unwarranted violence.

After his good deed, Daniel pressed on until he saw a large dry tree on fire. Creeping cautiously forward he found Squire trying to warm himself on the chilly December day. After their reunion the Boones probably trapped a while on the Kentucky before exploring the regions along the Green and Cumberland rivers. They were not alone. Early in the fall of 1770 a party of about forty Long Hunters had embarked for Kentucky under the leadership of Joseph Drake and Henry Skaggs. They were equipped with three packhorses for each man, rifles, ammunition, traps, dogs, blankets, and salt. By February 1771 only fourteen of the original hunters remained. Charles Ewing, who was said to be jealous of Henry Skaggs's superior success in hunting, may have previously exerted enough influence to lead off the rest of the group or they may have wearied of the wilderness. The camp of the remaining band was later raided by Indians supposedly led by Will Emery, a half-breed Cherokee. When the hunters returned, they carved the following inscription on a large beech-tree as a mute testament to their misfortune: *Fifteen hundred skins gone to ruination.*

Some of these Long Hunters—Henry, Charles, and Richard Skaggs, Casper Mansker, James Knox, James Dysart, William Miller, and two others—were likely among those who, according to one story, were once startled by a noise none of them could identify. Mansker told the others to keep still, grabbed his rifle, and glided into the woods to investigate. It could not be an animal since the noise came from a single unchanging direction. Could it be a new Indian trap? Mansker peered from behind a tree and saw a man stretched flat on the ground singing at the top of his lungs. Daniel Boone was entertaining himself while he waited for his brother to come back to camp.

The Boones joined forces with the Long Hunters for a short time, but left the Cumberland Valley for home in March 1771, with a fine load of furs. Sometime in May they reached Powell's Valley near Cumberland Gap. Here Squire came upon a skeletonlike creature whom he identified as his friend Alexander Neely. Neely had become separated from his hunting party and, bewildered and lost, had fired away all his powder hoping to attract his companions' attention. He survived on the meat of a stray dog that he managed to kill. Squire took Neely into camp and nursed him back to health with Daniel's help.

A portion of the Warriors' Path led through Powell's Valley and was too close for comfort to one of the Boones' nightly camps. One evening they were surprised while cooking their dinner by six or eight Indians, who accepted their invitation to share the meal. Soon the Indians proposed swapping guns—their worthless ones for the Boones' good rifles. Daniel and Squire refused and were set upon by the warriors, who stripped them of their skins, horses, rifles, and all their equipment. Told to go, they hid behind a log to observe the course the marauders would take, then hurried to a border settlement and raised a sympathetic band to pursue the thieves and try to recover the goods. A few miles beyond the camp, one of the whites shot a deer that had passed too temptingly near their route. The others, realizing that the report of the rifle had warned the Indians, thought it fruitless to continue the mission, and the Boones agreed. Their withdrawal was fortunate. They later learned that the small Indian band had been reinforced and was lying in ambush for the outnumbered whites just a mile or two ahead.

All the party except one who stayed with the Boones returned to the settlement. The remaining three stopped to spend the night in a deserted cabin and, glancing through the chinks in the logs a short while later, spotted two armed Indians bedecked in fine ornaments. They fired simultaneously and killed both Indians. Daniel and the unnamed companion each took a rifle as his booty; Squire took the silver trinkets.

A rifle and some jewelry—the last half year had been less than profitable for the Boones. Daniel had, according to Isaac Shelby, been "robbed of all the proceeds of this hunt of two years." The statement was not exact, for Squire had managed to bring back two packloads of skins and pelts. When Daniel arrived in the Upper Yadkin to greet his family, however, he was deeper in debt than when he had departed to find the Cumberland Gap. He could not help being greatly discouraged. Yet he had seen Kentucky. He had explored the land, knew it better perhaps than any other white man, and realized its potential. That was a great deal to think about.

4

TRANSYLVANIA AND THE WILDERNESS ROAD

VERY LITTLE INFORMATION has survived about the next two years in Boone's life. He farmed and hunted, each in its season. He often went hunting with an old weaver named Joe Robertson, who had a celebrated pack of bear dogs. They hunted in the Brushy Mountain and Watauga areas and once ventured as far as the French Lick (now Nashville) on the Cumberland before returning with a load of skins. Daniel no doubt also used these years to sound the Cherokees' willingness to sell Kentucky and became convinced that the country could be purchased. But Henderson's judicial appointment ran for another two years and effectively precluded his active involvement. Henderson urged patience; Boone chafed under the delay.

Daniel had changed his residence by 1772 to Sapling Grove in what is now Tennessee, but eventually moved back to the Yadkin. Store accounts indicate that his food purchases in Tennessee were for a family. They also dispel the contention of Boone's early biographer, John Mason Peck, that the pioneer never indulged in strong drink. An entry for January 26, 1773 read "2 quarts of Rum."

Boone reexplored Kentucky early in 1773 with Benjamin Cutbirth and a few other men. They camped in the same cave he had previously used on Little Hickman Creek and Daniel observed his custom of recording the visit by cutting his initials and the date into the cavern wall. He was again enormously pleased with the country and resolved to settle there without Henderson's help. On the way home he met Captain William Russell, the pioneer of the Clinch Valley, who became enthralled by Boone's descriptions of Kentucky and agreed to join him in attempting a settlement.

About August 12, James and Robert McAfee met Boone on their return from staking out land in Kentucky. They informed him that they were not alone in the endeavor. James Harrod's party and at least one other had been likewise engaged. In fear that all the best land would be taken before he even got under way, Boone redoubled his efforts to complete the necessary preparations. He recruited a number of his wife's relatives at the Bryan Settlement in the Lower Yadkin and rushed back north to sell his farm and whatever goods could not be transported easily. Five neighboring families joined him. They departed for Kentucky on September 25, 1773. For the sake of speed, the Bryans would meet them in Powell's Valley. Also, in this way the most dangerous part of the journey would be traversed together.

The migration involved extraordinary difficulties. The route was a serpentine hunter's trace which was too narrow for a wagon. A single-file packtrain of horses carried their provisions. Some of the party rode; most walked. Near Powell's Valley, Boone decided that he needed more flour and dispatched his son James along with John and Richard Mendinall to Captain Russell's at Castle's-woods to procure it. Russell provided the flour and sent some farming implements and a few cattle as well. His seventeen-year-old son Henry, Isaac Crabtree, a young man named Drake, and the family slaves, Charles and Adam, were sent to assist in conveying the goods. Russell, accompanied by Captain David Gass, would hasten to overtake the party as soon as his business was completed.

On the night of October 9, young Boone and Russell and their party camped on Walden's Creek, unaware that Daniel's company was but three miles ahead. At daybreak they were attacked while asleep by a force of Indians, who had tracked them most of the preceding day. Drake and one of the Mendinalls were killed outright; the other Mendinall crept off, mortally wounded. Crabtree, although wounded, escaped back to the settlements. Charles, the older slave, was captured and later tomahawked to death. Adam hid in some driftwood piled on the creek's bank to become an unwilling audience for the ensuing grizzly spectacle. James Boone and Henry Russell had both been shot through the hips and were unable to move. James recognized one of the warriors, a Shawnee named Big Jim, who had been a frequent visitor at the Boones' farm, and begged him to spare his life. He soon begged him to end it. The boys' bodies were slashed and stabbed countless times, with great care taken not to injure a vital organ, and their toe- and fingernails were torn out. A merciful death finally ended their ordeal.

Meanwhile, a petty thief, who had been apprehended with goods stolen from other members of Boone's party, decided to desert. He left before sunrise, paused long enough to pilfer a few deerskins Daniel had left by the trace for James to bring along, and headed for home. Reaching Walden's (now Indian) Creek just after the Indians had left, he dropped the skins and dashed back to the camp with his tragic news. Daniel organized the people to repel a possible attack and sent Squire with a few men to bury the dead and ascertain the strength of the enemy. Squire arrived on the scene to find Captains Russell and Gass staring in disbelief at the mangled remains of the boys. The dead had not been scalped. The Indians would not bring white scalps into their towns in time of peace. James and Henry were buried together, wrapped in a linen sheet provided by Mrs. Boone.

The distraught settlers held a general council in the main camp. Boone was the only one who voiced a strong desire to push on. The expedition was disbanded. Boone accepted Captain Gass's offer to stay temporarily in a cabin on his farm near Castle's-woods, probably hoping to convince Gass and Russell to make another try to reach Kentucky.

Daniel's dream seemed to be slipping out of his grasp. The McAfees and Harrod were only the first to explore Kentucky in the summer of 1773. George Washington traveled down the Ohio to Fishing Creek, where George Rogers Clark was already located. Simon Kenton and fourteen others were examining northeastern Kentucky. Captain Thomas Bullitt, Hancock Taylor, James Douglas, and James Smith were all surveying and claiming the choicest lands that they could find. It would be nearly eighteen months before Boone cut the Wilderness Road through to Boonesborough.

The boundary set by the Proclamation of 1763 was by this time academic. There was virtually no enforcement of its prohibition of western settlement. It had also become increasingly clear that the Ohio Valley could not be settled without a war with the Shawnees who were, at least in one sense, caught in the middle of a land grab by Pennsylvania and Virginia. George Croghan and his associates, as well as other Pennsylvania merchants, knew that their trade would be disrupted by any conflict. They were also attempting to colonize large areas of Pennsylvania and western Virginia (including eastern Kentucky), some of the same land which Virginia claimed for its veterans of the French and Indian War. The supporting forces of the Virginia surveying expeditions in Kentucky began to attack Shawnee hunting parties, and Lord Dunmore, the royal governor of Virginia, sent militia as further protection for its citizen-surveyors on the frontier. The Pennsylvanians accused their competitors of attempting to destroy the Indian trade; the Virginians countercharged that Pennsylvania merchants had purchased goods stolen from them by the Indians and had incited the Shawnees to try to drive them from the Ohio Valley.

Many historians have pointed to the fact that the conflict with the Indians, termed Lord Dunmore's War, virtually commenced with the murder of young Boone and Russell. Their fate was the talk of the frontier. In an unusual action, two Indians were eventually executed for the crime by their own chiefs, bowing to extreme pressure from the Virginia colonial government. The undeclared war which had existed along the borders since 1764 escalated as both sides committed the most inhumane acts to avenge previous atrocities. By early 1774 in Kentucky "no questions were asked on either side—but from the muzzles of their rifles." The event which precipitated all-out hostilities was the murder of the family of Tahgahjute, a famous chief who gave himself the English name of Logan. On May 1, 1774, Daniel Greathouse persuaded some friendly Indians to come to the white settlement near Yellow Creek, got them hopelessly drunk, and then shot them all. Among the group were Logan's brother and pregnant sister or sister-in-law. One or more of the Indians were scalped. The braves who attempted to cross the creek to help their comrades were driven back with numerous fatalities, and the unborn child was cut from its mother's womb and impaled on a stake. Indians had no monopoly on cruelty.

News traveled slowly on the frontier. When Daniel Boone set out in May to visit his son's grave he had not heard of the massacre of Logan's kin. He found that James's grave had been disturbed by wolves but not opened. While he finished recovering the plot he was caught in a violent storm. Nature seemed to support the melancholy associations the place held for him. He was more depressed then, he said, than at any other time in his life. He was startled out of his reverie by the noise of Indians approaching. Daniel escaped and ever after credited the storm with saving his life by delaying his pursuers.

By the time of Boone's return, Captain William Russell had received orders from Colonel William Preston, on the authority of Governor Dunmore, to choose "two faithful woodsmen" to warn the Kentucky surveyors of their imminent danger. Russell replied to Preston, "I have engaged to start immediately on the occasion, two of the best hands I could think of—Daniel Boone and Michael Stoner." He had immense confidence in Daniel. On July 13, he wrote again to Preston about the surveyors, "If they are alive, it is indisputable but Boone must find them."

One story concerned with this trip has been preserved. On their way to Kentucky they stopped at a place near the Blue Licks where the buffalo had licked away so much of the salty ground that deep trenches separated only by a narrow ridge had been formed. Stoner peeked through a small hole in the partition and saw a buffalo calmly feeding on the salt. Stoner, a Pennsylvania German, said to Boone, "Shtop, Gabtain, and we will have shum fun." Stoner removed his hat and thrust his head through the aperture into the face of the buffalo. But the buffalo was not frightened off. Instead, it rammed the wall and burst through the clay bank up to its shoulders. Stoner wheeled and screamed as he ran "Schoot her, Gabtain! Schoot her, Gabtain!" Daniel saw that Stoner was in no danger and fell to the ground convulsed with laughter.

They made their way along the North Fork of the Kentucky River to the Big Lick, where Boonesborough was later located, and reached Harrodstown before July 8. Thirty-four men were engaged in laying out the town. Each settler was granted "a half-acre in-lot, and a ten acre out-lot." Boone may have paused a short time to register as a settler and to erect a double cabin with Evan Hinton. The cabin, which was more likely built in 1776, straddled the boundary line between their two lots and satisfied the conditions of the settlement agreement for both men. Proceeding toward the mouth of the Kentucky, they found and warned Captain John Floyd's party, who agreed to turn back after finishing some surveying. Boone and Stoner pushed on to the Falls of the Ohio and warned another group of surveyors of the Indian threat before returning to the Clinch Valley on August 26. In sixty-one days they had traveled over eight hundred miles and had successfully notified the majority of the surveyors of their danger. Only a few of them were unable to escape.

Upon his return, Boone was commissioned a lieutenant in the colonial forces. He raised a party of recruits and marched off to the front, a defensive line which roughly extended from the mouth of the Kanawha River northward to Fort Dunmore (old Fort Pitt). He was recalled only two days later to help defend the Clinch region against a number of bloody Indian raids. Boone was an active commander. Captain Daniel Smith's record book noted the following: "Sept. 22d. Lieut. Boone, fourteen men, four days, three pounds of beef per day." Standing orders were to issue meat only to scouts or those in pursuit of Indians. Boone was quickly promoted to captain and was given command of Blackmore's and Cowan's forts, in addition to that of Moore's Fort, his previous responsibility.

Daniel's opposition was the formidable Logan himself. The avenging chief's war party waylaid three of Boone's men who had injudiciously gone 300 yards out of Moore's Fort to check pigeon traps. Boone and his other men arrived just after the shots were fired, but were too late. One man, John Duncan, had already been scalped. Boone pursued the raiders but with no success. He did so again the next month with the same result.

Boone's part in the war, and that of the other commanders of frontier forts, was to maintain a successful defensive posture; they were to react rather than act. The overall strategy of the campaign against the Indians was designed and initiated by Lord Dunmore. On July 24 Dunmore notified General Andrew Lewis that he himself would go to Fort Dunmore to reinforce the defenses of the upper Ohio, gather a strike force of one thousand men from the Monongahela and upper Potomac regions, and march down the Ohio River. Lewis was to march west along the Kanawha River with militia raised from Augusta, Botetourt, and Fincastle counties, combine with Dunmore's army at the Ohio, and together they would invade the Indian territory.

Cornstalk, a Shawnee chief who was an excellent general and tactician, knew that his only chance for victory against the enemy columns, either of whose force was numerically superior to his own, was to attack before they could unite. At dawn on October 10 he led a war party of eight hundred or more Shawnee, Mingo, Delaware, and Ottawa braves against Lewis's advance guard near Point Pleasant. Even when Lewis ordered the remainder of his troops into the battle, the result was at first a standoff. When Isaac Shelby led a flanking movement against the Indians, however, Cornstalk mistakenly determined that his worst fears had come true—either Dunmore's army or reinforcements from Augusta and Botetourt counties had arrived. He ordered a retreat. Lewis's losses of eighty men wounded and forty-six killed were probably comparable to those of Cornstalk. Since the Indians as a rule bore away the bodies of their dead, no exact figures concerning casualties could be determined.

The defeat of the Indians at Point Pleasant was of great importance because it indicated to both the Indians and the Virginians that Dunmore's offensive would be successful. Cornstalk told his people that they had two alternatives—kill their women and children and fight to the death or treat for peace. They decided to negotiate. In the same month Dunmore's agreement with the Indians, the Treaty of Camp Charlotte, established the Ohio River as the boundary line between the two groups. Concurrently, Dunmore decided to strengthen the frontier by garrisoning seventy-five men at the fort which bore his name and by erecting Fort Blair at the mouth of the Kanawha River. Traders and speculators were overjoyed. They now had a strong foothold in the Ohio Valley and the protection of forts.

Boone and his men were discharged from the militia by November 20. His employer, Richard Henderson, was no longer on the bench and felt the time was now ripe for his grand land scheme. In the autumn of 1774, he and Captain Nathaniel Hart visited the Cherokee nation and confirmed Boone's reports that Kentucky could indeed be purchased. Henderson's Transylvania Company wished to buy twenty million acres of land, nearly all of the present states of Kentucky and Tennessee, and to found the fourteenth colony, to be called Transylvania, with the company's officers as proprietors. Proprietary rights allowed the charging of an annual quit-rent on each acre of land sold, a guaranteed perpetual income. Henderson and his partners, however, were flouting the Proclamation of 1763 and the claims of North Carolina and Virginia to the territory. The royal governors were irate and, had it been any other time, would have demonstrated their displeasure by the use of troops. But talk of revolution was becoming more frequent. They could not afford to commit any more of their forces to the frontier.

Matters progressed swiftly in Henderson's and Hart's meeting with the Cherokees. February or March was set as the time for the groups to meet at Sycamore Shoals on the Watauga River to sign a treaty. An old, wizened chief, Attakullakulla (Leaning Wood), renowned for his wisdom, accompanied the Transylvania partners to Cross-Creek (now Fayetteville, North Carolina) to examine the goods offered for the land. The merchandise was shipped to the Watauga on December 6. By Christmas, Henderson had widely publicized his desire for "settlers for Kentucky lands about to be purchased."

Boone had used the winter to tour the Cherokee towns and to urge the inhabitants to attend the treaty. A thousand to twelve hundred Indians came to Sycamore Shoals in March. Daniel's role was that of negotiating the boundaries of the purchase. He was sure enough of the completion of the sale to have begun assembling woodsmen at the Long Island of the Holston River to cut the Wilderness Road.

Although no inventory has survived, the goods were said to have "filled a house." They were set in plain sight of the Cherokees and proved to be the most persuasive bargaining tool that Henderson possessed. Henderson originally anticipated no dissent and was taken aback when Dragging Canoe, an influential young chief, spoke out vehemently against the treaty. His keen eye had seen that the treasure offered, the equivalent of 10,000 pounds sterling or about $50,000, was not a fair price for the land. His speech caused a breakdown in negotiations. The next day, March 16, Dragging Canoe and the other opposing chiefs gave in to the demands of the young braves for the finery and some quantity of ammunition that stood tantalizingly before them. The treaty-deed was signed on March 17, 1775. It granted "Henderson and company the tract of country from the mouth of the Kentucky or Louisa River to the head spring of its most northerly fork, thence south-easterly to the top of Powell's Mountain, and thence, first westerly, and then north-westerly, to the head spring of the most southerly branch of the Cumberland River, and down that stream, including all its waters, to the Ohio, and up the Ohio to the mouth of the Kentucky." It was justly called "The Great Grant." Henderson then stated that he wished to purchase a right-of-way from the Holston River to "The Great Grant" and was prepared to offer "the value of two thousand weight of leather" and to pay the Indians' debt to John Carter of some six or seven hundred pounds. After some brief haggling, these terms for "The Path Deed" were also agreed to.

When the merchandise was doled out, there was much grumbling among some of the young warriors. One, whose share was a shirt, complained loudly that on the land sold he could have killed more than enough deer in one day to pay for this garment. Henderson wisely signaled the beginning of the feast he had promised the Cherokees. Many cattle were killed and roasted, and the rum, previously withheld, flowed freely.

At one point early in the negotiations, when the purchase seemed sure, Boone was taken aside by Dragging Canoe and told: "Brother, we have given you a fine land, but I believe you will have much trouble in settling it." To this prophetic chief was also attributed the remark that "There was a dark cloud over that country." No one recognized how true the two statements would prove to be. Boone, undaunted, left for the Long Island of the Holston to mobilize his axmen before the treaty was ratified. A road needed to be cut to Kentucky.

Thirty armed backwoodsmen warmly greeted Boone's arrival. Among those present were Squire Boone, Michael Stoner, Benjamin Cutbirth, Colonel Richard Callaway, David Gass, William Bush, Captain William Twitty, and Felix Walker, who chronicled the expedition. On March 10, 1775, the woods began to resound with the ring of axes. Blazing the trail through Powell's Valley and Cumberland Gap, they widened the Warriors' Path for approximately fifty miles before heading westward for a short distance near Hazel Patch, and then following a buffalo trace northwest to the Rockcastle River. "On leaving Rock-castle," according to Felix Walker, "we had to encounter and cut our way through a country of about twenty miles, entirely covered with dead brush, which we found a difficult and laborious task." They then carved out a path along another buffalo trace for "about thirty miles through thick cane and reed" before eventually reaching the Kentucky River. Walker recorded that as the cane ceased, "a new sky and strange earth seemed to be presented to our view. So rich a soil we had never seen before; . . . turkies [were] so numerous that it might be said they appeared but one flock, universally scattered through the woods."

The roadmakers had experienced no Indian trouble. Henderson's larger party, complete with supplies for a settlement, was about one hundred miles behind. When Boone and his men camped on Taylor's Fork of Silver Creek on March 24, they were but fifteen miles from their final destination, the Big Lick near Otter Creek. A half hour before dawn they were startled from their sleep by war whoops and rifle fire. Walker and Twitty were badly wounded, and Twitty's slave was shot and fell dead into the campfire. Dazed and only partially awake, the other whites grabbed their rifles and plunged half naked into the forest. Walker crawled to safety. As the Indians rushed the camp to scalp Twitty, his bulldog seized one brave by the throat and threw him to the ground. A second Indian tomahawked the dog and both fled without their trophy.

Boone reassembled his men. Only a few horses were missing but Twitty and Walker could not be moved. While Boone nursed their wounds, he had his men erect some small cabins for shelter which they termed "Twitty's Fort." Twitty died, but Walker was soon well enough to be transported by litter.

Walker later recounted one additional event that occurred during the stay at "Twitty's Fort." While gathering kindling, Colonel Callaway's female slave saw a man peep cautiously from behind a tree. She screamed "Indians" and ran for the camp. Boone snatched his rifle and ordered everyone to take cover. Then the "Indian" announced his name. He was one of their own party who was unsure if the whites had regained control of the camp.

The events of the next few days are described in part of Boone's letter of April 1 to Richard Henderson: "On March the 28th, as we were hunting for provisions, we found Samuel Tate's son, who gave us an account that the Indians fired on their camp on the 27th day. My brother and I went down and found two men killed and *sculped*, Thomas McDowell and Jeremiah McFeeters. I have sent a man down to all the lower companies in order to gather them all to the mouth of Otter Creek. My advice to you, Sir, is, to come or send as soon as possible. Your company is desired greatly, for the people are very uneasy, but are willing to stay and venture their lives with you; and now is the time to *flusterate* their [the Indians'] intentions, and keep the country whilst we are in it. If we give way to them now, it will ever be the case."

By April 6, those of Boone's party who had not turned back arrived at their destination. Walker's narrative stated that the group followed Otter Creek northward "to Kentucky river, where we made a station, and called it Boonesborough, wherein was a lick with two sulphur springs strongly impregnated." The site was no doubt selected for its proximity to the river and creek and the salt lick, which would attract game, and for the fact that the area was a plain which would require a minimum of clearing. Walker also describes the scene that greeted them at the end of their journey: "On entering the plain we were permitted to view a very interesting and romantic sight. A number of buffaloes, of all sizes, supposed to be between two and three hundred, made off from the lick in every direction; some running, some walking, others loping slowly and carelessly, with young calves playing, skipping, and bounding through the plain. Such a sight some of us never saw before, nor perhaps ever may again."

They began to build Fort Boone immediately. The few cabins erected were located sixty yards south of the Kentucky River and fronted the river a little below the lick. Despite their recent trouble with the Indians, the whole party seemed to have become quite careless in their defense and kept watch only the first night after their arrival. Such instances of foolhardiness were not isolated on the frontier. Men who were weary from exposure and the labor of constructing a fort did not want to stand guard. In this particular instance Boone had little or no control over his men; they were independent adventurers who recognized his abilities as a leader but would not always obey his orders. This lack of discipline no doubt

47

contributed to the sad event that occurred: "On the fourth day, the Indians killed one of our men."

Meanwhile Henderson, who received Boone's letter on April 7, was snowbound twenty miles east of Cumberland Gap. His men had to build shelters for the wagons before proceeding with packhorses. Angrily Henderson watched more lightly outfitted settlers pass him by to claim his land. But in the next few days he counted over one hundred terrified faces rushing eastward, back to civilization. Indian raids and the fear of these raids were taking a heavy toll. A subsequent letter from Henderson to his partners in North Carolina revealed that the success of Transylvania hinged on Boone's abilities. "It was beyond a doubt that our right, in effect, depended on Boone's maintaining his ground—at least until we could get to him. . . . It is impossible to make the picture worse than the original. Every group of travellers we saw, or strange bells which were heard in front, was a fresh alarm; afraid to look or inquire, lest Captain Boone or his company was amongst them, or some disastrous account of their defeat."

It was essential that Henderson reassure Boone that his party was on its way. William Cocke offered to bear the message in exchange for 10,000 acres of choice land and a traveling companion. Henderson agreed but could get no one to volunteer on equal terms, so Cocke reluctantly agreed to go alone. The next morning was gloomy and so was Cocke, who was having second thoughts about his impending 130-mile journey. Noting Cocke's growing hesitation, Henderson "struck whilst the iron was hot, fixed Mr. Cocke off with a good Queen Ann's musket, plenty of ammunition, a tomahawk, a large cuttoe knife, a Dutch blanket, and no small quantity of jerked beef." Cocke reached Fort Boone without incident.

On Thursday, April 18, Henderson's force was met by Michael Stoner and three others, who had brought additional packhorses to assist them and "excellent beef in plenty." The entire party arrived at Fort Boone at noon two days later. Both groups were at once overjoyed and relieved. The next few weeks were spent in putting the fort site in better order. Its location was shifted to higher ground, land was cleared, and a

fort garden was planted. A great deal of time was spent surveying and arguing over the method of choosing plots. After much
contention and two drawings of lots for land, Henderson said
that "every body seemed well satisfied." There also were
pressing external problems to be dealt with. James Harrod and
party were busy erecting the settlement of Harrodsburg to the
west, and a group of land seekers led by John Floyd had located temporarily on Dick's River to the southwest. Henderson had his Cherokee deed, but Harrod and Floyd already
occupied the land. Fortunately, by May 9, after a few days'
talk, Harrod and Floyd left Fort Boone, or Boonesborough as
it was also called, and were evidently content. A general meeting to establish a government was scheduled for May 23 in
Boonesborough.

Each group needed to elect delegates to the convention. On
Saturday afternoon, May 20, Boonesborough chose Daniel and
Squire Boone, William Cocke, Richard Callaway, William
Moore, and Samuel Henderson as its representatives. Four
delegates each were likewise elected in Harrodsburg, St.
Asaph (Logan's Fort), and the Boiling Spring Settlement. The
"divine elm" at Boonesborough was their point of assembly;
its branches could shade a hundred people. The address with
which Henderson opened the meeting was a long, involved
harangue spiced with eighteenth-century oratorical devices
that gave ample testimony to his legal career. He stressed the
need for wise laws, especially to prevent the wanton destruction of game, and the need for courts and a militia.

The session, which lasted only four days, was quite produc-
tive. It officially designated Transylvania as the name of the
colony. The minister, Mr. Lythe, introduced "*a bill to prevent
profane swearing and Sabbath breaking,*" which must have
been quite forceful. The bill was sent to "a committee to make
amendments." The ancient rite of "Livery of Seizin" was performed by Henderson and John Farrar, who had been the
Cherokees' attorney at the Sycamore Shoals treaty: the sym-
bolic handling of a small patch of turf from Farrar to Henderson completed the formal transfer of lands. The Boones
prepared some significant bills which were voted into law.

Daniel brought in one bill "for improving the breed of horses" and another designed "for preserving the game." Squire followed suit by introducing a bill "to preserve the range." Henderson reported that the delegates "finished the Convention in good order."

On June 13, Daniel Boone departed to bring his family to Boonesborough. Since the birth of his daughter Lavinia in 1766, three more children had been added to the family— Rebecca (1768 or 1770), Daniel Morgan (1769), and Jesse Bryan (1773). Daniel set a rapid pace for he was soon to be a father again. His importance to Henderson's plans of empire was nowhere more potently underscored than in a joint letter written by Henderson and one of his partners, Colonel Luttrell, to their North Carolina associates: "We are informed that Mrs. Boone was not delivered the other day, and therefore do not know when to look for him; and, until he comes, the devil himself can't drive the others this way." All Henderson's grand schemes had to be placed in abeyance. The success of Transylvania was predicated upon the new settlers who would follow Boone. They always followed Boone. But Daniel would not budge until the baby arrived.

Little William Boone was probably born in early July, but survived just a short time. Somber moments were seldom long indulged by pioneer families. By the latter part of August the Boones, in company with twenty young men whom Daniel had recruited, had joined other prospective settlers in Powell's Valley. At the head of Dick's River the party separated, with some choosing to go to Harrodsburg. The rest, led by Boone, came into Boonesborough on September 6 or 7. It was always Boone's boast that his wife Rebecca and his daughters were "the first white women that ever stood on the banks of Kentucke river." By the eighth he was getting ready to stock a larder with meat. Henderson's books reveal a charge to Boone for two pounds of powder and twelve pounds of lead.

Later in September, Squire Boone shepherded in a number of Rebecca's relatives, and Colonel Callaway guided in his family together with another group of hopeful settlers. The latter party met with a band of Cherokees who were friendly enough to give the whites part of a buffalo which they had killed. About this time, a solitary pioneer and Indian fighter made his way to Boonesborough after spending a season near the present site of Washington, Kentucky. Simon Kenton was only twenty years old, but as a frontiersman he was said to be more than the equal of all save perhaps Daniel Boone. He was a most welcome addition to the settlement.

The migration to Boonesborough continued throughout the autumn of 1775. The frontier for some time remained isolated from the ramifications of events which occurred in the East. On April 19, the day before Henderson reached Fort Boone, the battles of Lexington and Concord took place. The Revolution had begun. On May 28, at the end of the Transylvania Convention, the Reverend Lythe is said to have read the prayer for the royal family for the first and last time at Sunday services in Kentucky. News of the trouble in Massachusetts did not arrive until the next day. Suspicion was later voiced about the inquiries made by certain visitors. Some believed that they were Tory spies, intimates of Governor Dunmore, who were making friends with the Indians and examining the defenses of the various outposts.

In August, while Daniel was on his way back to Kentucky with his family, Henderson, then in North Carolina, met with his partners to discuss matters concerning Transylvania. They voted Boone a present of 2,000 acres of land "for the signal services he had rendered to the Company." (Later when the company's claim to the territory was voided and the proprietors received a compensatory tract of 200,000 acres, no one remembered those "signal services." Ultimately Boone was left landless in Kentucky.) In other business, the proprietors paid careful attention to the drafting of a memorial to the Continental Congress in Philadelphia. Henderson and his partners, unsure of the outcome of the rebellion, produced a masterpiece of equivocation and fence-straddling. They wished "to be considered by the Colonies as brethren, engaged in the same great cause of liberty and of mankind." They expressed the hope "that the united Colonies will take the infant Colony of Transylvania into their protection." On the other hand, if America remained a dominion of George III, they noted that they could "by no means forget their allegiance to their sovereign" and hoped "that Transylvania will soon be worthy of his royal regard and protection."

Henderson and his associates certainly cannot be condemned for their vacillation. Many of the delegates to the Continental Congress were equally unsure of the future. In fact, upon the advice of leading members of Congress, the memorial was not presented. Congress had just petitioned the king and hoped for peaceful accommodation. To admit a fourteenth colony would have been an act of outright defiance.

But Daniel Boone, far removed from Philadelphia, had no time to wonder about the outcome of Congress's and the king's deliberations. His problems were immediate.

5

THE REVOLUTION ON THE FRONTIER

Most of December 1775 proved uneventful in Kentucky. The main occurrence was the opening of a Transylvania land office on the first of the month. The rush was on. Sadly, claim boundaries often overlapped unintentionally. Boone and others would suffer immense losses from these "shingled" claims. But that was in the future. For the time being, uninterrupted peace provided a sense of security. At first the Indians did not seem to notice the growing invasion of their territory. Not until December did the tribes north of the Ohio learn that large numbers of whites were constructing permanent settlements on their hunting grounds.

Two days before Christmas, Colonel Arthur Campbell, accompanied by two boys named McQuinney and Sanders, left the fort and crossed the Kentucky River to search out fertile bottomland. They separated, with Campbell going 200 yards upstream and the unarmed youths climbing a hill to reconnoiter. Ten minutes later the crack of a gun and a scream echoed through the forest. Rescuers rushed from the fort and met Campbell running to the landing with only one shoe on. He said that he "had been fired on by a couple of Indians" just 300 yards away. Boone raised a scouting party, but could ferret out neither the Indians nor the boys. Much concern was expressed for the dozen or so hunters who were absent and had no knowledge of the ambush. All of these men, however, gradually straggled in. No trace of the boys was found until McQuinney's scalped body was discovered in a cornfield three miles from the fort. Sanders was never found.

A party of rangers under Jesse Benton was dispatched the next day to determine if any Indian force was in the vicinity. They were given two shillings a day and offered five pounds for each Indian scalp they took. They returned on the thirty-first, convinced that the red men had retreated north across the Ohio. The raid seemed not to be part of any organized attack. At the October Treaty of Camp Charlotte, King Cornstalk of the Shawnees had spoken of a renegade band of warriors over whom he had no control. He stated that "if any of them should be killed by the whites, no notice should be taken of it." When the settlers finally learned of the treaty, they believed that these braves were the ones responsible for the incident. Those who could tried to push the whole matter into the backs of their minds. Many could not. The settlement of Kentucky had progressed quite well: almost 900 claims entered for 560,000 acres; 230 acres of corn raised; horses, cattle, hogs, and poultry introduced; and even 500 apple trees planted by Nathaniel Hart. But ammunition was running low. How long would the Indian treaties forestall open conflict? The pressure was too great. Soon, of the five hundred people that had ventured into Kentucky, only two hundred remained, twelve of whom were courageous women like Rebecca Boone.

Those who stayed were less than united. Early in 1776, Daniel and Squire Boone accompanied surveyors who were laying out a tract of 70,000 acres at the Falls of the Ohio for the proprietors. The action angered many of the settlers, who rightly regarded this land as probably the most valuable in Kentucky. There was also much bitterness over an increase in land prices from twenty to fifty shillings per hundred acres. As a result, a petition of grievances signed by James Harrod, Abraham Hite, Jr., and eighty-six others was presented to the Virginia Convention in April. To quell the ire of the discontented, who now took issue as well with the validity of the Transylvania Company's claim, Henderson announced that he

Daniel Boone, painted by John James Audubon sometime
after their meeting in 1810.
*Courtesy of John James Audubon Memorial Museum,
Henderson, Kentucky.*

"Daniel Boone Escorting Settlers Through the Cumberland Gap," by George Caleb Bingham. *Courtesy of the Washington University Gallery of Art, St. Louis, Missouri.*

Fort Boonesborough as it appeared before the siege of September 1778, from George W. Ranck's *Boonesborough* (Louisville, 1901). *Courtesy of the Filson Club, Louisville, Kentucky.*

A SCENE AS THE FRONTIERS AS PRACTICED BY THE HUMANE BRITISH AND THEIR WORTHY ALLIES!

Bring me the scalp
and the King our Master
will reward you!

Arise Columbia's Sons and forward press,
Your Country's wrongs, call loudly for redress;
The savage Indian with his scalping knife
Or tomahawk may seek to take your life.

By bravery aw'd, thro'll in a dreadfull fright
Shrunk back for refuge to the woods in flight.
Their British leaders then will quickly shake,
And for those wrongs shall restitution make.

Henry Hamilton, British governor of Detroit, known as "The Hair-Buyer," in a Revolutionary propaganda broadside. *Courtesy of the Museum of Northern Arizona, Earle R. Forrest Collection.*

The rescue of Jemima Boone and Betsey and Fanny Callaway, kidnapped from Boonesborough by Indians in July 1776. From William A. Crafts, *Pioneers in the Settlement of America* (Boston, 1877).

Simon Kenton, painted by Louis Morgan. From Samuel W. Price,
The Old Masters of the Bluegrass (Louisville, 1902).
Courtesy of the Filson Club,
Louisville, Kentucky.

A tree carving by Daniel Boone:
"D. Boon cilled a Bar on tree in the year 1760."
From Reuben Gold Thwaites, *Daniel Boone* (New York, 1902).

THE
DISCOVERY, SETTLEMENT
And present State of
K E N T U C K E:
A N D
An ESSAY towards the TOPOGRAPHY,
and NATURAL HISTORY of that important Country:
To which is added,
An A P P E N D I X,
C O N T A I N I N G,

I. The ADVENTURES of Col. *Daniel Boon*, one
of the firft Settlers, comprehending every important Occurrence in the political Hiftory of
that Province.

II The MINUTES of the *Piankafhaw* council, held at *Poft St. Vincents, April* 15, 1784.

III. An ACCOUNT of the *Indian* Nations in-
habiting within the Limits of the Thirteen U-
nited States, their Manners and Cuftoms, and
Reflections on their Origin.

IV. The STAGES and DISTANCES between
Philadelphia and the Falls of the *Ohio*; from
Pittfburg to *Penfacola* and feveral other Places.
—The Whole illuftrated by a new and accu-
rate M A P of *Kentucke* and the Country ad-
joining, drawn from actual Surveys.

By J O H N F I L S O N.

Wilmington, Printed by JAMES ADAMS, 1784.

Title page of John Filson's *Kentucke*, which contained the first
published account of Daniel Boone's life.
*Courtesy of the Filson Club,
Louisville, Kentucky.*

would not demand any money for the lands already sold until September.

About May 1, 1776, Colonels Henderson and Williams left to try to confirm their claim before the Virginia Convention and, if need be, before Congress. On June 15, the still embittered men of Harrodsburg elected Captains John Gabriel Jones and George Rogers Clark to serve as delegates to the Convention. They were to urge that the territory be organized into a new county of Virginia. On the same day, Henderson was presenting his case in Williamsburg. Nine days later the Convention proclaimed that the Cherokee purchase lacked their legislative approval and therefore could not be considered a valid claim. A near deathblow was dealt to the company's hopes on July 4, 1776, when the Convention appointed commissioners in eleven frontier counties to gather information negating Henderson's purchase. When the news of the Declaration of Independence reached Williamsburg, it sealed the fate of the proprietary colony of Transylvania. Henderson's sole salvation rested with Great Britain's fortunes of war. Any rapid resolution of the claim was most unlikely and, for a considerable period, the matter thus tottered precariously on the brink of disaster.

In the West the American War of Independence was mainly an Indian war. There were too few British regulars at Detroit and the several other scattered outposts to mount a significant offensive against the American settlements. They could, however, furnish supplies and leadership to the Indians of the Ohio Valley, who in many instances were all too ready to go on the warpath against those who had usurped or devastated some of their best hunting grounds.

Although other colonies such as Pennsylvania obviously participated in the Revolutionary War in the West, Virginia bore the brunt of the conflict. Its citizens formed the majority of the settlers and consequently the majority of the militia. The war was fought over lands they claimed in defiance of British law and of the claims of other colonies; to Virginians the war was a unique and special cause. When Henry Hamilton, the British Lieutenant-Governor, first arrived in Detroit in

November 1775, he accurately sized up the uneasy peace that existed between the settlers and the Indians in a letter to Governor Carleton in Quebec. He wrote that the Indians "are not likely to continue upon terms with the Virginians. . . . The savages have a high opinion of them as Warriors, but are jealous of their encroachments, and very suspicious of their faith in treaties." He also stated that the Virginians "have plundered, burnt, and murdered [the Indians] without mercy. Tis to be supposed from the character of the savages that opportunity only is wanting to retaliate and that there can be little cordiality between them."

Early in the struggle English strategists recognized the value of forcing the colonies to fight a war on two fronts. One such plot was even hatched before America declared its independence. John Connolly, Lord Dunmore's former Indian agent, received the permission of the British commander-in-chief General Gage to organize the Indians and frontier Loyalists and attack Fort Pitt. Simultaneously, Lord Dunmore, who had fled Virginia and sought asylum on a British man-of-war in Chesapeake Bay, was to lead an attack from the sea. Connolly would march to the east and Dunmore to the west. Between them they hoped to crush any resistance in Virginia. Fortunately, Connolly was such a well-known figure on the frontier that he was recognized and captured by Patriots before he could execute his plan.

The failure of grand schemes like Connolly's, however, did little to stop the British from effectively playing upon the Indian-settler antagonism of decades past. The brutal confrontation over the trans-Appalachian west commenced long before the Revolution and would continue long after the last echo of the shots "heard 'round the world" had ceased.

Incited by the British, the Indians now stepped up their raids on the northern settlements in the summer of 1776. A number of men were killed and several more were missing. Writing from the Holston country on July 7, Colonel Russell, sure of an impending Indian war, advised the immediate abandonment of Kentucky.

Boonesborough, however, had not suffered serious Indian

trouble since December. The people had become less and less cautious as they saw no evidence of any imminent threat. While to the east the Continental Congress was in Sunday session on July 14, attempting to provide men and supplies for Washington's army, the residents of Boonesborough were indulging the leisure activities of a sunny Sabbath day. Jemima Boone, Daniel's attractive daughter, convinced Betsey and Fanny Callaway to go with her on an excursion in the settlement's canoe. She wanted to soak her foot, which had received a painful "cane stab," in the cool river water. A young Virginian, Nathan Reid, promised to join them, but was too busy to do so at the last moment. The three young women felt quite capable of managing the dugout alone. Betsey, sixteen, was engaged to Samuel Henderson, and Fanny and Jemima, both fourteen, had more than their share of serious suitors.

They pushed off from shore with the Callaway girls paddling easily along and Jemima trailing her foot in the stream. Nearing a prominent rocky cliff on the northern shore, the girls realized that the current had drawn them about one-fourth of a mile below the fort. Unalarmed, one of the Callaways suggested going ashore to pick wildflowers and young cane. Jemima half-heartedly objected to landing on the Indian shore, saying that she was afraid of the Indians, whom she called "the *yellow boys.*" They decided to turn upstream and go home. The current, however, much stronger near the cliff, drew them close to the shore despite their strongest exertions. The thicket of cane and bushes rustled and then suddenly parted in an explosion of painted warriors. One dashed waist deep into the water, seized the buffalo tug on the prow of the canoe, and tried to drag the vessel ashore. Fanny Callaway thwacked the eager brave over the head with her paddle until it broke. Her sister followed her example. When the other Indians reached their beleaguered brother, they made clear that they would capsize the boat if the beating continued. The screaming girls were pulled from the craft and hauled onto the shore. Their shrieks terminated abruptly when one warrior yanked back Betsey Callaway's hair and gestured with his knife that another sound would forfeit her scalp.

After being forced to climb the riverbank, Jemima refused to move. She pointed to the "cane stab" and declared quietly that she would rather die than march barefooted. Threateningly raised tomahawks did not persuade her to alter her decision. Jemima and Fanny were quickly given moccasins. The dresses of all three were cut off at the knees for rapid travel; the remnants were used for leggins. The Indians hurried them forward, anxious to put a good distance between themselves and the fort, and kept to the harder ground of the ridges to leave less of a trail.

Jemima knew one of the captors, a Cherokee named Hanging Maw, whom she had probably seen at her father's Watauga cabin. The others, three Shawnees and another Cherokee, were unknown to her. She knew that since they had already traveled out of earshot of the fort the Indians would now allow her to break the silence which they had previously demanded. Hoping they might be released, Jemima told Hanging Maw who she was, and when asked, answered that the others were indeed her sisters. Perhaps they would all be set free. Hanging Maw only laughed. By accident he had gotten the upper hand over the famous "Wide-Mouth." "We have done pretty well for old Boone this time," he said.

They camped six miles from the river, about three miles southwest of the present Winchester, Kentucky. The historian Draper noted that "As soon as they stopped, the captives were pinioned at the elbows, so that their hands could not touch each other; each of the captives placed beyond the others' reach, with one end of the tug with which they were tied, made fast to a tree, while the other was lain upon by one or more of the Indians, who sprawled themselves upon the ground in a circle around their prisoners." Anxiety made it impossible for the girls to sleep. Jemima tried to reach the penknife in her pocket, but she was bound too tightly.

The journey to the north resumed early the next morning. The girls knew they would be pursued and devised all manner of excuses for leaving a plainly marked trail. They broke twigs and bushes, and when caught, told the Indians that they were tired and had to pull themselves along. Betsey secretly shredded her linen handkerchief and dropped pieces of it strategically near their path. Until she had the heels knocked off her shoes by the Indians, she dug them deeply into every soft spot she could find. Jemima, blaming her wounded foot, frequently tumbled to the ground with a loud scream, praying that her voice might signal their location. At each of these instances tomahawks and knives were brandished in the girls' faces. The trio were quiet for a few minutes and then resumed their actions.

Despairing of making any good time with such weak and clumsy white squaws, the Indians happened that afternoon to find a stray pony. Here, they thought, was a way to increase their speed. Jemima, the most obvious offender, was placed on the animal. Fanny, and sometimes her sister, were also mounted behind her. They covertly kicked, pinched, and pricked the pony in every way possible to get him to rear or buck and followed the previous pattern of falling to the ground with a piercing yell. At first the Indians would merely put them back on the beast. The inevitable tumble kept occurring. One patient brave mounted the pony to demonstrate how easily it could be managed. The three were very slow pupils. The Indians, realizing that the use of the pony gained them no time, abandoned it in the woods. These must have been the most indulgent warriors ever to take prisoners. The girls' behavior was obnoxious enough to warrant death time and again by Indian code. Betsey Callaway was the only one disciplined—the frustrated pony bit her sharply on the arm.

That night's camp was a few miles south of Hinkson's Fork of the Licking River. The girls were given a meal of smoked buffalo tongue which was hard, unsalted, and barely palatable, before they were bound. By nine o'clock the next morning, Tuesday, July 16, the band was within thirteen miles of the Upper Blue Licks. A few miles further on, feeling completely beyond the reach of the whites, the braves shot a buffalo, cut out part of the hump, and cooked the first meal since the capture. Their assurance deepened the girls' gloom. Their relatives and friends should have overtaken them by now. It was three days since the abduction.

There was more vigorous activity on behalf of the young women than they realized. On Sunday, when the screams were heard at the fort, Daniel Boone leaped from his bed, seized his rifle, and ran down to the riverbank, not even pausing to take his moccassins. Little Caleb Callaway ran to the lick and alerted Captain Floyd and Nathan Reid who, hastening back, joined in the preparations already under way for pursuit. Samuel Henderson, Betsey's fiancé, dropped his razor in the midst of shaving and ran downriver with Boone. These two, Floyd, Reid, William B. Smith, John Gass, and others had to get the canoe set adrift by the Indians, since it provided the only quick way of crossing the river and keeping powder dry. John Gass fearlessly plunged into the water while the others flanked the shore with rifles cocked, ready to fire if any Indians should appear. Gass succeeded in bringing the craft back and crossed to the Indian side with Boone, Henderson, and three others. Colonel Callaway meanwhile led a mounted party a mile below Boonesborough to a place where they could ford the river. Boone divided his party to try to discover some sign of the Indians and their prisoners. Floyd's group found the trail first. Boone, turning back upriver, also came upon the trail and was soon met by Callaway's men. The agitated Callaway insisted on running down the marauders with his band, but Boone dissuaded him, knowing that the Indians usually posted one brave as a rear guard. At any alarm from him, the captives would be tomahawked. It was decided that Callaway's horsemen should proceed at full speed straight to the Lower Blue Licks to head off the Indians' retreat at the customary crossing point on the Licking River. Boone and his men would cautiously pursue the general direction of the trail on foot.

Floyd's men had already followed the tracks about five miles before night and Boone overtook them. A dog barked. Boone and others moved slowly forward to investigate and found nine men engaged in building a cabin who had not been molested by the Indians. After concluding to camp here, they evaluated their condition. There was little ammunition, no provisions, and no proper clothing. One's best Sunday pantaloons were hardly suited to the task at hand. The intrepid John Gass made a round trip journey back to the fort in the darkness of night, and returned with hunting attire, jerked venison, and Daniel Boone's moccasins.

At Monday's first light, Boone's party, bolstered by three of the cabin builders, resumed the pursuit and soon reached the spot where the Indians had camped. Beyond the camp the trail disappeared. The kidnappers had temporarily separated and, taking full advantage of thick canebrakes, had vanished without a trace. Daniel vetoed the idea of fanning out and attempting to follow whichever trails might be found. It would waste crucial time. He was sure that the Indians were aiming for the Shawnee towns on the Scioto, and insisted on striking off to the right and taking a northerly route parallel to what he felt was their true course. They crossed the trail a number of times and, finding the encouraging signs which the girls had left, redoubled their pace until nightfall forced them to halt.

Decamping at dawn on Tuesday, by ten o'clock they came to Hinkson's Fork. Boone believed that the Indians would have forded the stream just below them. A journey of 200 yards proved him right. The water was still muddy and the moccasin tracks still fresh. Daniel decided to follow directly on the trail again, since the Indians had traveled thirty-five miles with no sign of pursuit and would probably be less cautious. For the most part, the braves used the Warriors' Path, which led toward the Upper Blue Licks. They would sometimes take a buffalo trace to break the trail, but inevitably returned to the path.

Boone and his men broke into a trot and after eight or nine miles came upon a recently slaughtered buffalo. Blood was still oozing from the hump where the Indians had taken the choicest cut of meat. Daniel predicted that the Indians would stop to cook a meal at the first water. A mile or two further on the pursuers found a small snake, which the Indians had crushed, still writhing. The trail stopped at a stream. The warriors had evidently waded along the creek bed, but no tracks left the water in the vicinity. Boone knew they were close. It was noon and it was likely that the braves were preparing their meal somewhere next to the stream.

Daniel had previously ordered his men to maintain silence. His gestures now reinforced the dictum that no sound be made. He motioned the party to divide. Henderson, Reid, and others went downstream, while Boone, Floyd, and the remaining men went up the creek. Daniel's advance scout, probably William B. Smith, soon halted and waved the others forward. The camp was only thirty yards away. Before they could reach him, they saw Smith fire and miss. The Indians had spotted him, he said, and he was trying to drive them away from the captives. Boone and Floyd fired hurried, but eventually mortal, shots as soon as they were within range of the retreating braves who, although alerted by Smith's shot, were unprepared to repulse an attack. Hanging Maw had just taken a kettle to bring cooking water from the stream, one was gathering wood, another preparing the meat, and the sentry had left his post to light his pipe from the newly kindled fire. Boone's men gave a loud yell and rushed the camp. One warrior flung a tomahawk at Betsey Callaway before he dove into the cane. It barely missed her head. The girls, who had been sitting on a log, jumped to their feet at the first rifle crack. Jemima joyously screamed, "That's Daddy!" They began to run toward their deliverers. Boone commanded them to fall flat on the ground in case the Indians might fire upon them. But the girls quickly bounded up again as the white men took the camp. In the confusion, one man mistook Betsey for an Indian because of her cutoff dress, makeshift leggins, and the red bandanna wrapped around her head. He was about to club her with the butt of his gun, when Boone grabbed his arm and exclaimed, "For God's sake don't kill her when we have travelled so far to save her from death!" When the fellow realized what he had almost done, he wept like a child.

The reunion was so emotional that if the Indians had returned the whites would have been at a terrible disadvantage. But the surviving warriors were happy to escape. They left knives, tomahawks, some moccasins, and two small shotguns, which were smashed over a tree as worthless. Recovering his composure, Daniel pointed to a bush, stating that there "I fired at an Indian." Drops of blood and a rifle were found at the spot indicated.

When the girls calmed down enough to speak, they told of how their English-speaking captors had bragged about the Cherokee war parties supposedly assembling on the Kentucky and near the Upper Blue Licks, and about the disturbances in the Watauga region. With this knowledge, Boone determined to set out for home as soon as possible. Strangely, no further word was heard of such a war party. The whites went just a few miles before making camp. Both girls and rescuers were exhausted from their ordeal.

Along the way back to Boonesborough, the party encountered the same pony which the girls had used to vex the Indians. This time the animal was quite docile when pressed into service. As they neared the fort, they were overtaken by Callaway's mounted band. The horsemen had left the Blue Licks after discovering the tracks of a solitary retreating Indian. They surmised that the braves had been routed and the girls rescued, and had proceeded home. July 17, when all returned, was a day of joy at Boonesborough.

On the return trip, and no doubt inside the fort as well, Samuel Henderson was the object of many jokes with a three days' growth of beard on half of his face and several additional days' on the other. It did not seem to dampen Betsey's ardor. On August 6 or 7, they were the first couple to be married in Kentucky. Daniel Boone officiated as magistrate under Transylvania authority. Colonel Callaway consented to the match only after exacting an oath from Henderson that the marriage would be solemnized by a more recognized authority as soon as possible.

The adventure of the three girls caused a sensation on the frontier. The story was as eagerly received on the seaboard and further heightened Daniel Boone's reputation as a wilderness scout and Indian fighter. Years later, James Fenimore Cooper used the episode as the basis for the captivity and rescue of Alice and Cora Munro in *The Last of the Mohicans*, and the main character of his Leatherstocking Tales always seemed to bear a strong general resemblance to Boone.

A few days after the Henderson-Callaway wedding, a traveler brought a copy of the *Virginia Gazette* to Boonesborough. It contained the first news of the Declaration of Independence. Eastern politics and turmoil did not yet play a major role in the thinking of Kentuckians, however. In the summer and fall of 1776, Boone commented in his "autobiography" not upon the continuing struggle for independence from Britain, but that the Indians had "attacked several forts, . . . doing a great deal of mischief." There were no major attacks, but successive raids took their toll upon the feeble Kentucky settlements. Seven stations broke up. Only Boonesborough, Harrodsburg, and McClelland's Station remained. Palisades were begun at each of the three outposts, but as the alarm subsided they were completed only at McClelland's Station. The concentration of the two hundred settlers in three locations did have a beneficial effect. Three forts could be defended more easily than the previous ten.

Ammunition was running low. In early July, before the capture of the girls, George Rogers Clark and John Gabriel Jones, the delegates to the Virginia Convention from the western parts of Fincastle County, left for Williamsburg to ask for support. When they arrived, they found a new constitution for a new state, a new government in operation, and a new governor—Patrick Henry. The Convention, however, had adjourned. Clark visited Governor Henry at his residence in Hanover County and then went on to Williamsburg to try to convince the Executive Council of Kentucky's importance to the defense of Virginia. The Council was hesitant at first to supply stores, already having a war on its hands, but granted the determined Clark five hundred pounds of powder on August 23.

Meanwhile, Major Arthur Campbell of Holston sent a limited supply of powder and lead to Kentucky. On September 7, Captain Boone reported that he had sold all of it to the people at six shillings per pound for powder and ten pence per pound for lead, except for a small amount reserved for scouts. In justice to Henderson and his associates, it should be noted that during most of 1775 and 1776 they provided the powder and shot for the entire countryside. According to Draper, "These accounts remain unclosed upon the books in every instance, shewing a condition of no little indebtedness for the colonists of Transylvania to the great proprietors."

The Transylvania Company's claim to Kentucky was soon repudiated by the Virginia legislature. Captains Clark and Jones laid a petition before that body, and although they were not given seats, a bill was introduced at their request on November 7 to form the county of Kentucky out of the area incorporated as Fincastle County, Virginia, in 1772. Although Henderson's vigorous opposition delayed passage of the bill for one month, on December 23 county officers were appointed. John Bowman became the first official Kentucky colonel, though Boone may have held the title under Henderson's authority. Clark was made a major of militia and Boone a captain.

Clark and Jones had already left to descend the Ohio from Pittsburgh with the precious supply of powder. Noting a continued Indian presence, Clark secreted the cargo in various places near Limestone (now Maysville, Kentucky) and set their boat adrift. He went to Harrodsburg for reinforcements while Jones and some other men remained at Hinkson's deserted settlement. Jones, joined by John Todd and others, concluded that ten men were a sufficient force to convey the stores to the settlements, and set out to retrieve them. They were ambushed and defeated on Christmas day five miles east of the Lower Blue Licks by a band of forty or fifty Mingoes under the command of the notorious Pluggy. On December 29, Pluggy attacked McClelland's Station. Luckily, Clark had just arrived with the men from Harrodsburg on his way to get the powder. The Indians were repulsed and Pluggy was among their dead.

Simon Kenton and a companion trailed the remnants of Pluggy's raiding party back to the vicinity of Limestone and remained in this dangerous area long enough to be sure that the caches of powder were still safely hidden. Later Kenton returned to the settlements and then went out with about thirty men to bring in the powder. He refused to allow the group to use the shorter but more exposed Warriors' Path on the homeward trip. If the powder was lost, so was Kentucky. They returned safely by a longer route.

About the same time, in January 1777, the settlers abandoned McClelland's Station, fearing that another attack was imminent. Only Boonesborough, Harrodsburg, and perhaps Price's Settlement on the Cumberland were yet occupied. The entire number of men fit for duty in the country was not much more than one hundred and fifty. The bloody time, remembered afterwards as "the year of the three sevens," had begun.

Irate over the defeat of Pluggy, Blackfish, war chief of the Shawnees, took it upon himself to rid Kentucky of all whites. In a February 27 letter asking Patrick Henry and the Council of Virginia for aid, Captain Hugh McGary stated: "We are surrounded with enemies on every side; every day increases their numbers." The first strong war party ever seen near Boonesborough was assembled in early March. During this month, however, it was Harrodsburg that suffered most. On March 2, four young men were ambushed near there by seventy of Blackfish's warriors. Thomas Shores was captured and William Ray was killed and scalped. William Coomes managed to hide in a treetop and observed the disfiguring of Ray's body. James Ray, the dead boy's brother, outran all of the warriors and escaped. Towards evening, thirty settlers on horseback went in search of their missing friends. McGary blanched at the sight of the mangled remains of his stepson. When one man mistakenly identified the body as that of Coomes, he was startled as the "dead" man came out from cover exclaiming "No, they haven't killed me, by Job! I'm safe!" But at least three other men from Harrodsburg fell victim to the Indians that month.

On March 7, a detachment of Blackfish's force killed a black field hand at Boonesborough. The outlying settlers now came in to "fort up." All was fairly quiet until April 24. Early that morning Daniel Goodman and a companion, who had left the fort to drive in some horses, were fired upon. They fled toward the stockade, but Goodman was tomahawked sixty or seventy yards from the gate. Simon Kenton, who was just setting out on a hunt, killed the Indian about to scalp Goodman. Boone and a dozen others rushed out to help Kenton pursue the retreating braves and ran straight down a path between two fields. Kenton killed a warrior who had Boone in his sights. By the time he reloaded, he saw that a large number of the hundred hidden Indians had circled behind them. Boone recognized their extreme peril and yelled "Boys, we are gone—let us sell our lives as dearly as we can!" He ordered a charge through the enemy to the fort. Each man fired once and then clubbed down anything in his way with his gun. Boone's left ankle was broken by an Indian shot. Kenton killed the Shawnee who tried to tomahawk Boone, clubbed down another brave who was after Daniel's scalp, and then picked Daniel up and ran for the fort. As the pair neared the palisades, they were assisted in by Jemima Boone, who darted out of the fort to help.

As was usual with even a large Indian raiding party, Blackfish and his braves retreated once the element of surprise was lost. The chief knew that there was little chance of taking a fortified settlement defended by Kentucky long rifles and that even if their attack was successful they would pay too great a price in warriors' lives. There would be other and better opportunities to capture Boonesborough.

When the whites were safe inside the fort, their wounds were dressed. The ball extracted from Boone's ankle had flattened as it hit the bone. Daniel sent for and thanked the young man who had saved his life three times that day in a disarmingly understated fashion: "Well, Simon, you behaved like a man to-day: indeed you are a fine fellow." The painful wound disabled Boone for a number of weeks, and ever after served as an unpleasant barometer for the weather or fatigue.

Boone knew that there would soon be a major shortage of food. He divided the people into two companies—one to act as guards and scouts, the other to plant and cultivate corn. On May 23, or perhaps July 4 (the date is uncertain), the reflection of the sun from an Indian's rifle revealed the secret approach of a war party eventually estimated at two hundred braves. All the whites fled to the fort. Three were wounded before they reached it. The Indians besieged the compound for two days before giving up in disgust and contenting themselves with destroying whatever cattle they could find. Boone's sharpshooters had decreased the number of Blackfish's war party by seven.

Indian raids continued, but sustained, full-scale attacks were few. Half-truths spread along the frontier that "Boone was badly wounded" and "the people of Kentucky were penned up in forts." These rumors may have helped persuade Virginia to send reinforcements to Kentucky. Colonel Bowman arrived on August 1 with one hundred men. Captain William Bailey Smith had gone to the Yadkin and returned on September 13 with forty-eight of Boone's kindred and friends. They entered Boonesborough single file, keeping six feet between horses to give the illusion of a larger force. The ruse worked—Indian scouts reported the arrival of two hundred white warriors. Blackfish and his band now relegated themselves, in Boone's words, to practicing "secret mischief." Indian marauders were now aggressively pursued by parties of armed whites.

Nevertheless, in his "autobiography" Daniel Boone could truly state for the people of Kentucky that "we passed through a scene of suffering that exceeds description." The suffering would apparently continue. The Indians had destroyed cattle and crops. Food was scarce and it was too late to plant. It seemed that starvation might succeed where the tomahawk had failed. In December, Colonel Bowman wrote from Harrodsburg to General Hand at Pittsburgh requesting corn. If none could be sent, he said, he expected to "do without bread till we can get it from what we intend to plant." Boonesborough, however, had a partial source of grain. The previous year's cornfield, unlike the new fields, had not been burned by Blackfish. In some instances spillage and natural seeding produced seven or eight barrels to the acre. This situation was probably the source of the now famous remark, made some years later by General Charles Scott, concerning the fertility of Kentucky's soil. "If planted," said he, "and cultivated as you Virginians do yours, twenty barrels would be an ordinary yield; if planted and not cultivated, ten barrels; *and if not planted at all, seven barrels!*"

Life became more hopeful but certainly not easy. There was no reason to believe the Indian attacks would cease. Even when Daniel Trabue arrived in Boonesborough on Easter Sunday, 1778, the situation had changed very little. He noted that "the people in the fort was remarkably kind to us with what they had, but I thought it was hard times, no bread, no salt, no vegetables, no fruit of any kinds, no ardent spirits, nothing but meat." But without salt, none of the fresh meat could be preserved. This vital ingredient was essential to the survival of the Kentucky settlements.

6

CAPTIVITY AND SIEGE

On January 8, 1778, Boone and thirty men set out for the lower salt spring of the Blue Licks. They were to be the first of two contingents from Boonesborough to make salt for the Kentucky settlements. The normal trip to the North Holston wells would take too long, given the weakened state of the settlements. Boonesborough's own salt lick, created by a sulphur stream, would not produce salt for human consumption. The government of Virginia had, at Colonel Bowman's request, provided the large kettles in which to boil down the briny water. The water at the Blue Licks was weak; 840 gallons were necessary to make one bushel of salt. That bushel, however, commanded a formidable price—a cow and a half. The large force of men was required not so much to work the boiling operation as to prevent Indian attack. Licks were a favorite spot for all hunters because of the game they attracted. But winter was an unlikely season for trouble.

Unfortunately for Boone and his party, this winter would prove far from typical. The previous June the American Brigadier General Edward Hand had arrived at Fort Pitt for the purpose of consolidating defenses on the upper Ohio, but could not follow through on his plan to attack the Indian villages of the Wyandots and of the Pluggy's Town confederacy. The successful raids of the Indians—their September 1 assault on Fort Henry, in which twenty-three of the garrison were killed, and the ambush later that month of Captain William

Foreman's scouting party, in which he and twenty of his men died—forced Hand to use what troops he had to defend vulnerable perimeter areas.

British officials coordinated the intensification of Indian attacks. Governor Hamilton of Detroit was particularly adept at playing upon the tribes' hatred for the white settlers. Within six months after July 1777, when he dispatched fifteen well-supplied war parties to the frontier, he reaped a bounty of 129 scalps and 77 prisoners. Although British plans for the year had been stymied by Burgoyne's defeat at Saratoga on October 17, the news of his surrender did not slow Indian attacks in the West. Their fury was fired by a particularly brutal action on the part of the Americans. That same October, King Cornstalk, accompanied by two other Shawnee chiefs, Old Yie and Redhawk, had come to Fort Randolph to tell the Americans that their tribe was yielding to British pressure and the chiefs could no longer urge neutrality. The commandant, Captain Arbuckle, had no wish to hurt the chief who had proved faithful to his treaties in the past, but, faced with this declaration, held the three hostage. He later also detained Cornstalk's son, Elinipsico, who came to the fort searching for his father.

One morning in early November a soldier from the garrison was killed and scalped close to the fort by Indians. The captain of his company, a man named Hall, burst by the protesting Arbuckle with a group of his men and savagely murdered the four captive braves. The Shawnees needed no further justification to become allies of the British.

Such events made the Kentucky settlements one of the first lines of defense in the West. But the ability to hold Boonesborough and the other forts would be in some respects proportional to the success of Daniel Boone and his party at making salt.

Several weeks passed after their arrival at the licks with no remarkable occurrence. Daniel appointed himself one of the hunter-scouts for the party, and on February 7 he left camp with a packhorse to get a supply of meat. This occupation gave him a chance to keep a check on his string of beaver traps as well. He had to go ten miles below the Lower Blue Licks to bring down a buffalo. Snow was falling heavily by the time he had butchered the carcass and fastened three or four hundred pounds of meat to his horse with strips of buffalo hide cut from the animal.

Satisfied with the kill, he started back for camp. After traveling through a narrow path past a fallen tree, his horse spooked. Looking over his shoulder, Daniel saw four Indians coming at him. The fast-falling snow had muffled their movements. He furiously tried to throw off the meat and escape on horseback but found that the buffalo tugs had frozen. He reached for his knife to cut the straps but could not draw it from its scabbard. It too was frozen fast; he had forgotten to clean the blood and grease off the blade. All this took but a moment. With no option other than surrender, the forty-four-year-old Boone took to his heels. But the Shawnees were young and swift. After a half mile, their warning shots kicked up the snow on either side of Boone. One brave had cut loose the meat and was pursuing Boone on his own horse. The next shot cut the strap of Daniel's powder horn. He knew there would be no further warning. Exhausted, he dodged behind a tree and placed his rifle in front of it as a token of submission. "Wide-Mouth" had been captured.

Ushered back to their nearby camp, Daniel was stunned at what he saw: over a hundred fully armed Shawnees painted for war, with Blackfish himself in command. Even worse, there were whites to help direct the attack—two Frenchmen in British employ, and two "white Indians," James and George Girty, the brothers of Simon Girty, the terror of the frontier. As the traditional amenities of the handshake and "How d'do" greetings were observed with the chiefs, Boone recognized his old captor from 1769. Daniel accosted him by name: "How d'do, Captain Will?" No Indian was more astonished than Captain Will at this greeting. After he was reminded of the encounter by Boone, he shook hands again with increased cordiality. Following his lead, each chief repeated the ritual.

Blackfish then came forward with Pompey, a renegade black who served as his interpreter, and informed Boone that he was on the march against Boonesborough. The unusual winter expedition was meant to avenge the murder of King Cornstalk and his companions. The war chief then asked Daniel if the salt-boilers were his men. Boone evaded the question until he was told that Indian spies already knew their number and location. He acknowledged that they were his. Blackfish stated in a matter-of-fact tone that he would kill them. Daniel was thinking fast. He had to divert the attack from Boonesborough. Most of the defenders were making salt, no attack on the settlement was expected, and the fort still lacked one wall. The case of his own men was equally hopeless.

Daniel decided to try a bit of duplicity. He said that he would persuade his men to surrender if the Indians promised that they would be well treated and exempted from running the gauntlet. He also said that all of his people would be happy to live with the Shawnees, but that the women and children would not survive a winter march. He offered to accompany the warriors to the fort in the spring to arrange a peaceful surrender. Blackfish agreed, but noted that if Boone did not convince the salt-boilers to give up he would forfeit his own life.

At noon the next day the Indian force arrived at the Blue Licks. They surrounded the salt-makers and remained undiscovered only 200 yards away. The men, seeing Boone and others approaching, thought the relief column from the fort was at hand. Then they saw the Indians. As they leaped to their feet and snatched up their rifles, Boone yelled "Don't fire!—If you do, all will be massacred!" He explained the situation and persuaded them to surrender. Twenty-six additional prisoners were thus taken. Two scouts and two salt-packers were absent. Boonesborough would be warned.

An Indian council was convened to determine the fate of all the prisoners except Boone, who was needed for the spring capitulation of the fort. Such a betrayal of trust seemed impossible to Boone. The action, however, was the repetition of what American soldiers had done to Cornstalk and his party. Pompey was allowed to translate the two hours of deliberations for Boone in a low voice. Blackfish also let Daniel make the closing speech, an indication that he wished to keep his word despite the protests of many braves. Boone's plea, as

73

recorded later by one of the salt-boilers, gave his men the first hint that their lives hung in the balance. He addressed the Indians saying: *"Brothers!*—What I have promised you, I can much better fulfil in the spring than now. Then the weather will be warm, and the women and children can travel from Boonesborough to the Indian towns, and all live with you as one people. You have got all my young men; to kill them, as has been suggested, would displease the Great Spirit, and you could not then expect future success in hunting nor war. If you spare them, they will make you fine warriors, and excellent hunters to kill game for your squaws and children. These young men have done you no harm, they were engaged in a peaceful occupation, and unresistingly surrendered upon my assurance that such a course was the only safe one for them; and I consented to their capitulation on the express condition that they should be made prisoners of war and treated well. I now appeal both to your honor and your humanity; spare them, and the Great Spirit will smile upon you." Pompey translated the speech sentence by sentence to the Shawnees. The vote was taken. Fifty-nine were for sacrificing the prisoners and sixty-one for sparing them.

The British agents argued to no avail for an attack upon the weakened fort. Preparations were made for the return march. Three hundred bushels of salt were dumped into the snow. The plunder was divided and a load designated to each white. Boone refused to carry the large brass kettle that was his portion. A brave shoved it at him. He returned the shove so violently that both the Indian and the kettle were sent whirling to the ground. At this point, Blackfish interposed to take Boone under his special care. His partiality to Boone, when combined with Boone's speech, aroused suspicions of the pioneer's loyalty among the captives. Boone never had the opportunity to divulge his plans to them.

At that night's camp, Boone noticed some braves clearing a hundred-yard path in the snow. He took Pompey with him and gently complained to Blackfish about the promise that his men would not run the gauntlet. Blackfish replied: "O Captain Boone, this is not intended for your men but for you." Boone

74

had forgotten to include himself in the exemption. Indians armed with tomahawks, clubs, and switches formed two lines six feet apart along the path. Boone stripped to the waist and began the race. He ran in a zigzag pattern that gave few braves a chance to inflict a severe blow. One brave near the end of the line, who was determined that Daniel should not pass unscathed, stepped directly into the path. Daniel pretended not to notice him and, at the last moment, butted the fellow full in the chest with his head and ran over him to safety. The Indians roared at their companion's discomfort and complimented Boone as a "vel-ly good so-jer."

Although the two missing scouts, Flanders Callaway and Thomas Brooks, soon made known the disastrous capture of the salt-makers to the people of Boonesborough, little could be done. Kenton and others followed the trail to the Ohio before giving up.

The march to the Shawnee towns lasted ten days and was described by Boone in the "autobiography" as "an uncomfortable journey, in very severe weather." He added that they "received as good treatment as prisoners could expect from savages." They arrived at Old Chillicothe on the Little Miami River on February 18. This many prisoners had not been taken since the defeat of Braddock's forces in 1755. Despite Daniel's protests, all the other captives were now forced to run the gauntlet but fortunately no one was seriously hurt. Soon Boone and sixteen of his men were adopted into the tribe, with Boone having the good fortune to be adopted by Blackfish; he was truly highly regarded by the Indians.

Daniel was given the name "Shel-tow-ee" or "Big Turtle." One of Boone's early biographers, John Mason Peck, who had had a number of conversations with the frontiersman, described the adoption ceremony: "The hair of the head is plucked out by a tedious and painful operation, leaving a tuft, some three of four inches in diameter, on the crown, for the scalp-lock, which is cut and dressed up with ribbons and feathers. The candidate is then taken into the river in a state of nudity, and there thoroughly washed and rubbed, 'to take all his white blood out.' This ablution is usually performed by females. He is then taken to the council-house, where the chief makes a speech, in which he expatiates upon the distinguished honors conferred on him, and the line of conduct expected from him. His head and face are painted in the most approved and fashionable style, and the ceremony is concluded with a grand feast and smoking."

On March 10, Boone accompanied Blackfish to Detroit to sell to the British the ten prisoners who had not been adopted. Of this exploit, Boone said that "During our travels, the Indians entertained me well; and their affection for me was so great, that they utterly refused to leave me there with the others, although the Governor offered them one hundred pounds Sterling for me, on purpose to give me a parole to go home."

Governor Hamilton, known as "The Hair-Buyer" because he gave rewards for American scalps or prisoners, obtained permission to interrogate Boone and from him received confirmation of Burgoyne's surrender. He urged Boone not to tell the Indians. "You are too late, Governor," Daniel answered, "I have already told them of it." Boone was said to have shown Hamilton his old commission from Lord Dunmore as a British captain and to have hinted that the Kentuckians might be won over to the British cause. These developments undoubtedly sparked Hamilton's desire to ransom Boone. Blackfish, however, would not part with his "son," even for five times the usual bounty for captives. He had plans for Shel-tow-ee. Daniel was the key to the taking of Boonesborough.

Before departing for Chillicothe, Boone, who had previously refused similar private offers from sympathetic English gentlemen, did accept a horse, saddle, bridle, and blanket from the governor, as well as some silver trinkets to use as Indian currency. His good treatment by the British was an indication that they believed he would influence Kentucky to support the crown. Some of the American prisoners also began to share that belief. On April 10, Blackfish and his "son" left for home. Along the way, the chief stopped to notify a number of Delaware, Mingo, and Shawnee villages of the time of assembly at Chillicothe for the grand expedition against Boonesborough.

When they returned, they discovered that one of the captives, named Andrew Johnson, who had led the Shawnees to believe that he was a fool, had escaped. Johnson had feigned fear of entering the forest alone and had demonstrated such severe gun-shyness that his lack of marksmanship was the laugh of the camp. The Indians felt that he was not smart enough to escape and paid him little heed. In actuality Johnson was a veteran frontiersman who was soon leading retaliatory raids against the Indian towns. Boone later declared that bringing the salt-boilers to the Indian villages was a crucial mistake for the Indians. For the first time a number of Kentuckians knew the location of the Shawnee camps.

The "autobiography" recorded that Daniel fit in well with his Indian family and tribe: "I was exceedingly familiar and friendly with them, always appearing as cheerful and satisfied as possible, and they put great confidence in me. I often went a hunting with them, and frequently gained their applause for my activity at our shooting-matches. I was careful not to exceed many of them in shooting; for no people are more envious than they in this sport." Boone was eventually permitted to hunt alone, but received a carefully limited supply of powder and shot. By using light loads and sometimes recovering the spent balls, he was able to amass the supply of ammunition he felt he needed to escape. Once he stocked a rifle for one of his tribesmen and received more ammunition as a payment. He also requested a flint, ostensibly to test the gun, but which readily found its way into his cache of ammunition, lock, and rifle barrel.

By June the Indian army began to assemble for the Boonesborough assault. When returning from salt-making on June 16, the Shawnee band scared up a flock of turkeys near the present Xenia, Ohio. The braves pursued them about three-quarters of a mile until the birds landed in some trees. Busy shooting the turkeys, they were unaware that Boone had escaped. Daniel cut the lashings that held the brass kettle to his horse and answered his "mother's" agitated questions about his actions by stating: "I am going home; I must go and see my squaw and children, and in a moon and a half, I will bring them out here to live with you." As he said goodbye, the squaws raised a loud yell which made him urge his pony forward at the best possible speed.

He rode all that night and did not slacken his pace until his horse gave out at ten o'clock the next morning. He turned the pony loose and put the saddle, bridle, and blanket in a tree with the thought that they might prove useful to someone. He pushed on, frequently breaking his trail by running on trees which had fallen perpendicularly to his route. Reaching the Ohio near the end of day, he swam the river, pushing before him a small raft he had made to carry his clothes and belongings. Another story says that he crossed the river in an abandoned canoe he happened upon.

After a sound sleep, he treated his "scalded" feet with an ointment prepared by pounding peeled oak bark into a jamlike ooze. He also cut down a sourwood sapling, carved a rough stock for his gun barrel and tied the barrel and lock to the stock, using the thongs which secured his blanket to his back. He was quite proud of his new rifle's accuracy and soon brought down a buffalo, which supplied him with an excellent repast. According to the "autobiography," Daniel arrived at Boonesborough on Saturday, June 20, "after a journey of one hundred and sixty miles; during which I had but one meal."

On his return he found that Jemima, who had wed Flanders Callaway, was the only family member who had not gone back to North Carolina. All had thought he was dead. Daniel could not indulge his loneliness, however. During the four and one-half months of his captivity little progress had been made on the defenses of the fort. Boone animated the settlers with the news of the impending attack and directed their hasty preparations. One side of the fort was still not enclosed with palisades; two additional blockhouses had to be built; the gates needed strengthening; a new well had to be dug inside the fort; and the brush and stumps outside the stockade, which

78

would provide excellent cover for the Indians, needed to be cleared. The most pressing improvements were completed in ten days and meanwhile some reinforcements came from Logan's Fort and Harrodsburg. The suspense was unbroken until July 17, when William Hancock, a recent escapee from Chillicothe, brought word that the Indian expedition had been delayed three weeks because of Boone's escape. Blackfish had sent runners to Governor Hamilton to apprise him of the new situation.

Boonesborough was at the ready but the war party did not come. In the "autobiography" Boone said that "the Indians had spies out viewing our movements, and were greatly alarmed with our increase in number and fortifications." He suspected that the reports of these scouts were the real reason for the delay in attacking, and toward the end of August he determined to head a raid against Paint Creek Town on the Scioto to take Indian prisoners and gain information. Colonel Callaway bitterly opposed the plan, for he had doubts about Boone's motives and loyalty. But Boone prevailed. Thirty volunteers set out on August 31. By the time they reached the Blue Licks, eleven had decided to turn back. Boone, Kenton, and the others continued on.

As usual, Kenton took the point. When within four miles of their destination he heard a bell tinkle, hid himself, and soon discovered two Indians, one riding, one walking. The Indian on foot suddenly jumped on the back of his friend's pony, greatly startling him. Both laughed. Both were now lined up in Kenton's sights. He fired, killing one and badly wounding the other with a single shot. When he ran up to take their scalps, he heard the cane rustle behind him and just as he dove into the brush, two balls whistled past his head. More warriors came up, but so did Boone and his men. In the ensuing battle two more of the thirty or forty Indians were wounded and all their baggage was taken. The settlers sustained no injury.

These Indians had been on their way to join the main attack column. The absence of braves from Paint Creek Town told Boone what he wanted to know—the attack force was on the

79

move. He made all possible haste to return to Boonesborough before their arrival while Kenton and another man decided to stay to try to secure horses or a prisoner. Boone's party slipped by the Indians at the Lower Blue Licks on September 5 and got to the fort the next day. The inhabitants now frantically cleaned and repaired guns, molded and trimmed bullets, brought in vegetables, and filled all available containers with water.

The war party arrived about ten o'clock on September 7, a beautiful Monday morning. Boone put the Indians' number at 444 and the French Canadians' at an even dozen. Pompey advanced under a flag of truce and hailed Boone, asking him to come out to receive letters from Governor Hamilton. Boone hesitated until Blackfish called out to Shel-tow-ee to come and meet him. Daniel went forth to Pompey and both went to a designated stump to confer with Blackfish. After a handshake and initial greetings, Blackfish asked: "My son, what made you leave me in the manner you did?" "I wanted to see my wife and children so bad, that I could not stay any longer," replied Shel-tow-ee. "If you had let me know," said the chief, "I would have let you go at any time, and rendered you every assistance."

Blackfish then reminded his son of his promise to deliver the fort, and presented a letter and proclamation from Hamilton. The message was that the people would be taken to Detroit, become British subjects, and be well treated, and that any officeholders should be continued at the same rank. The alternative was a massacre. Blackfish asked how Boone liked the terms. Daniel answered that he had been kept a prisoner for so long that new commanders had been appointed and he must first consult with them. Blackfish agreed and then mentioned that his warriors were hungry. Boone, who knew they would take whatever they pleased, kept up the pretense of friendship saying: "There, you see plenty of cattle and corn; take what you need, but don't let any be wasted." He went back to the fort as the Indians began killing cattle and gathering corn.

In the discussion inside the fort, Daniel stated that he

preferred to fight, but would abide by the decision of the majority. Squire Boone, who had become something of a Baptist preacher, said hotly that "he would never give up; he would fight till he died." All the men agreed. "Well, well," mused Daniel, "I'll die with the rest." They also agreed to try to stall the negotiations to gain time. Help should be coming from Virginia.

Boone and Major William B. Smith went out to treat with Blackfish, Moluntha (who had replaced the slain Cornstalk), and the Canadian commander, De Quindre. A panther skin was spread over a log to serve as a seat for the diplomats from Boonesborough and bushes were held over their heads to shade them from the sun. Blackfish addressed them, again urging the capitulation of the garrison. He exhibited a wampum belt with three rows of beads—black symbolizing a warning, white emblematic of peace, and red for the blood that would flow if resistance was encountered. Blackfish said that one end of the belt represented Detroit and the other Boonesborough. Which row or path would the whites choose?

Smith evaded the question by remarking that it would be very difficult to transport the many women and children to Detroit. "I have brought forty horses," countered Blackfish, "on purpose for the old people, women and children to ride." Boone asked for the rest of that day and the following one to confer with the many white commanders. Blackfish granted the request and agreed on a line thirty yards from the fort over which neither side would pass. He even presented Daniel with a gift of seven jerked buffalo tongues for the white squaws as a token of good faith. Some believed the meat to be poisoned, but such was not the case. The interview ended with both sides smoking together in friendship with each group unknowingly being covered by an opposing band of riflemen.

The next day the people of Boonesborough tried to create the impression that the fort contained many defenders. Actually, there were sixty individuals who could bear arms, forty of whom were effective. But Blackfish had brought forty horses to transport the women and children; he probably had believed Boone's inflated figures of the garrison's size. To encourage this belief the women were dressed in surplus hats and hunting shirts and, armed with rifles, marched back and forth in front of the fort's open gate. That evening Blackfish demanded their decision. He was shocked by Boone's reply that his people refused to go to Detroit and would defend the fort to the last man. Shel-tow-ee sarcastically thanked his "father" for the extra time to strengthen the settlement's fortifications. Unexpectedly Blackfish offered to negotiate a treaty and peaceful withdrawal of his army with nine white representatives. Boone eagerly grasped at the additional time and remarked that the proposition "sounded grateful to our ears."

At length a place sixty yards from the gates was selected for the next day's meeting. During the conference Squire Boone stated, much to the consternation of the Indians, that George Rogers Clark was leading an army to Boonesborough—a false tale but one very disturbing to the braves present. Daniel and his friends vigorously protested Blackfish's demand that he be accompanied by eighteen Indian deputies. He said that number was necessary so that each town would be represented; otherwise the treaty would not be considered binding. The white men returned to the fort knowing that they would be outnumbered two to one on the morrow, and fully expecting the worst. Although the Indians' original offer was probably a genuine one, the last was extremely suspect. Blackfish was seen walking slowly around the palisades and scrutinizing the fort's defenses. The Shawnees even performed a war dance. Neither of these actions bolstered confidence in Blackfish's sincerity.

On the following morning, Wednesday, September 9, the negotiations were renewed. Few Indians were visible. After sharing a sumptuous meal prepared by the ladies of the fort to demonstrate their "vast" store of foods, young warriors replaced the older counselors at the talks. When Boone objected, he was told by Blackfish that the change was made at the request of the warriors, who wished to witness the historic proceedings. With such a switch, Boone must have been glad he had given explicit orders that twenty-five of his best sharpshooters man the bastions with their rifles cocked. At the first sign of hostility, they were instructed "to fire at the lump." He was gambling. The odds were two to one that an Indian would be the victim.

When all were seated, the peace pipe was passed and Blackfish proposed that they "forever bury the tomahawk, and live as brothers should live." Boone replied that he was willing and asked what terms would be stipulated. The war chief said he would give the settlers six weeks to leave Kentucky, for they had no right to the land. The whites refused and reminded him of the treaty with the Cherokees. Blackfish pretended not to have heard of the document, but when its existence was confirmed by a Cherokee who was present, he said that "that entirely alters the case; you must keep it, and live on it in peace." He then set the Ohio River as the boundary between whites and Indians which was not to be crossed with hostile intent. Hunting, trading, and trapping were to be permitted on either side of the river. The only other demand was that the people of Boonesborough take the British oath of allegiance. After some discussion these stipulations were accepted.

Blackfish said that he had to make a speech to inform his men that a firm peace had been made. After he concluded, he went up to the white commissioners and cautioned them not to be afraid for it was customary, he said, at the conclusion of a treaty that was to be long and lasting, that they shake "long hands," a grip in which two Indians embraced each white man in a way that brought their hearts close together. Blackfish and another brave advanced toward Boone and the other Indians paired off similarly with each white. The handshake turned out to be a grappling hold. Blackfish yelled "Go!" An Indian on the perimeter of the treaty ground fired a signal shot and all the braves now tried to drag the whites down a clay embankment a few yards distant, out of range of the fort's guns.

The attempt failed. The immediate volley from the fort's sharpshooters killed one Indian and so disconcerted the others that the settlers were able to break free. The fact that Boone had thrown his "father" to the ground hard enough to stun him added to their confusion. Daniel was struck by an Indian wielding a pipe-tomahawk as he was about to dash for the fort. The handle cut a two-inch gash across the back of his head and the blade inflicted a lesser wound between his shoulders. Squire was hit by a bullet and knocked down, but jumped up and ran for the gate. It was shut. He and John South then ran to a previously designated cabin door to gain the relative safety of the fort. It was estimated that the Indians secreted all around the treaty ground fired 200 rounds at the fleeing whites. Squire was the only one seriously hurt. In a slack moment Daniel cut the ball out of his brother's shoulder. Squire was forced to retire to his bed, but took a light broadax with him, vowing to use it as long as he could if the Shawnees penetrated the fort.

The first shot from the bastion was fired by William Stafford. He had drawn a bead on a chief sitting a bit beyond the treaty council and had squeezed the trigger at the Indians' signal shot. The ball was fatal. But a number of Indians had been thinking along similar lines. Ambrose Coffee had carelessly stretched himself out on an upper log of the bastion to view the treaty. At the first fire, fourteen balls pierced his clothing. Incredibly he tumbled into the compound unhurt, receiving no small amount of abuse for his foolhardiness.

Daniel Boone had an encouraging word for everyone as he made his rounds of the garrison. Only then did he have his wounds dressed. The Indians' first charge was repulsed. Unfortunately, the settlers had not had time to clear the shrubs and trees from around the fort to lessen the available cover. The smell and smoke of gunpowder soon permeated the air. An old Dutch potter named Tice Prock could not bear the odor, or perhaps the danger, and was discovered by Mrs. Callaway hiding under a bed. She encouraged him to his duty with her broomstick and ousted him from his next haven under the bellows of Squire Boone's smithy. Daniel Boone and Colonel Callaway intervened at this point and upbraided Tice for his cowardice. He was told to finish digging the new well if he would not fight, and he did so with commendable zeal—the deeper he dug, the safer he would be. At a lull in the fighting, Callaway noticed that Tice had left the well. Questioned,

Prock replied that he would not work while others did nothing. Callaway, who ordered him back to digging, became infuriated when the potter refused, drew his tomahawk, and chased Prock about the compound until he jumped back into the well and dug at a furious rate for a considerable time.

When the Indians saw that two days of constant fire produced no tangible results, they pursued some new schemes. They scattered flax along a fence that was connected to the fort and set fire to it, hoping that the flames would spread to the nearby blockhouse. The men inside foiled their design by tunneling under the palisades and pulling down the section of fence near the wall. The Indians then tried to lure the people out of the fort by pretending to withdraw, but the racket they made "departing" assured the settlers that all that was in store for them outside the gates was a deadly ambush. The people of Boonesborough outwaited the Indians, who, realizing that their ruse had failed, began once again to bombard the fort with a seemingly limitless supply of powder and shot.

On September 11 the muddied water of the river revealed a new tactic. De Quindre had convinced the braves to dig a mine from the riverbank to the palisades sixty yards distant. The settlers quickly erected a rough observation tower on the roof of the cabin which had originally served as Richard Henderson's kitchen. They could now see the dirt being thrown into the river and adopted the only practical defense—a countermine. It was begun in Henderson's kitchen, ran parallel to the river, and was dug two or three feet wide and ten feet deep. The severest fighting since the beginning of the siege occurred that night. Rapid flashes from the rifles completely lit up the interior of the fort. Boone ordered a ceasefire just before daybreak to conserve ammunition. The Indians followed suit.

The Shawnees were especially careful not to expose themselves after the building of the watchtower. Pompey, however, constantly popped his head up near the opening of the mine to observe the fort. A few ineffectual shots were fired at him. William Collins, an excellent marksman, took careful aim at the place where Pompey's head had last emerged and fired the instant his head came up. Pompey was neither seen nor heard from again. Another version of Pompey's demise stated that he was perched in a tree sniping at the inhabitants of the fort and that it was Boone, using "Old Tick-Licker," his favorite rifle, who dispatched him. The episode may be inextricably confused with one described by Draper in which an Indian, not Pompey, was firing into the fort from a tree. The brave varied his attack by "pulling up his breechclout, and exhibiting his person in a bantering, derisive manner." Boone's "Tick-Licker," which carried a one-ounce ball, was pressed into service, given an extra charge of powder, and put an end to the striptease. Presumably it was Daniel who pulled the trigger.

This same morning Boone had a box rigged to dump their excavated earth over the stockade walls to inform the attackers that the appropriate measures to nullify their mine were under way. John Holder and others picked up large stones as they were dug up and heaved them over the palisades and down the riverbank at the Indians. Irate curses verified their aim. Old Mrs. South, a simple soul, begged Holder "not to throw stones at the Indians, for they might hurt them, make them mad, and then they would seek revenge." Her remark became a byword among the men, who parodied it in many a sarcastic taunt and jeer flung at the Indians.

The enemy worked at the mine unceasingly and in several days penetrated two-thirds of the distance to the fort. The settlers, both on the battlements and in the countermine, could hear them digging and would sometimes bawl out to the Indians, "What are you doing down there?" "Digging a hole," they replied. "Blow you all to hell before morning, may be so! And what are you doing?" "O, as for that," rejoined the settlers, "we are digging to meet you, and will make a hole large enough to bury five hundred of you sons of bitches!" Providentially for the beleaguered whites, it rained almost every night during the siege. A particularly heavy downpour eventually caused major cave-ins in the Indian mine and forced them to resort to their rifles. They again took full advantage of the fort's ill-chosen location to fire down upon the compound from the river bluff and the hill southwest of the lick. One spent ball struck Jemima Boone Callaway as she was standing in her cabin doorway. She was facing inside to help supply her father with ammunition and had exposed what most biographers have gallantly referred to as "the fleshy part of her back." An adjustment of her undergarment was sufficent to make the bullet, which had barely penetrated the skin, fall out. The Indians did manage to sever the flagpole and cheered as the American colors fell to the ground. The men in the fort soon took down the pole, reattached the flag, and raised a loud cheer as they set their standard back in its place.

Squire Boone, who was something of an inventor, had made his own preparations for the siege by constructing a wooden cannon from a tough black gum tree. Although it was reinforced with iron bands, it cracked at its first trial. He then made another which was tried twice and found effective. Squire waited for a good target. One morning he spied a large group of Indians some 200 yards from the fort. The cannon was brought out and loaded with a swivel cannon ball and twenty bullets, then aimed and fired. The Indians scampered in all directions. Several were thought to have been killed or wounded. But either at this discharge or the next, the barrel cracked and the weapon was useless. Anticipating also that the Indians would attempt to burn down the fort, Squire had unbreeched several old musket barrels and fitted them with pistons which would force out from a pint to a quart of water. The squirt guns were given to the women so they could extinguish any fire arrows or torches which lodged on the cabin roofs. The roofs sloped in toward the fort for greater protection and were covered with long shingles, each fastened only with a single peg. A sharp blow with a pole from within a cabin would usually dislodge a flaming shingle if the squirt guns failed to quench the fire.

For several nights while digging the mine, the Indians did try their best to burn the fort. It was fortunate for the settlers that the roofs were kept damp by the nightly rains. Some of the fire arrows had a small quantity of powder tied in a rag attached to them, which was ignited by a crude time fuse made of punk. Such arrows would set a number of shingles ablaze. Still, the settlers were safely able to knock them loose. Extinguishing the torches thrown against the stockade was another matter. Often it could be done only by going outside the fort. John Holder took such a risk to douse a torch thrown up against a cabin door. He seized a bucket of water, flung open the door, and put out the blaze, roundly cursing the Indians the entire time. Mrs. Callaway heard him and he came in for a protracted tongue-lashing from the pious woman, who could tolerate his profanity little more than Tice Prock's cowardice.

On Thursday night, September 17, the Indians made a final unsuccessful effort to set fire to the fort. Their war whoops as they rushed the stockade and flung the torches at the cabin roofs were answered by the defiant yells of the whites within. It was again so bright that it was said a pin could be seen anywhere within the fort. William Patten, or Patton, who was out hunting when the Indians appeared, viewed this incredible scene at a distance—the repeated attacks of the Shawnees with their torches, the screams and yells from within the settlement—and concluded that the fort was taken and its inhabitants massacred. He hastened to Logan's Fort with his sad news. Benjamin Logan prepared his people for the battle which he was sure would come. Only a few straggling Indians, however, were encountered.

Almost no Indians could be seen near Boonesborough on the morning of the eighteenth. They were retreating gradually, hoping to keep up the pretense of the siege. Soon all had departed and the victorious settlers emerged from their quarters for the first time in nine days. Some of the men procured cabbages to feed the half-starved cattle that had been penned up within the stockade; others picked up the bullets on the ground outside the walls. British lead could be melted and recast into American bullets. In the "autobiography" Boone said that they "picked up one hundred and twenty-five pounds weight of bullets, besides what stuck in the logs of our fort." The bastion nearest the river was said to have an additional hundred pounds of lead embedded in it. Daniel also summarized the battle statistics: "we had two men killed, and four wounded, besides a number of cattle. We killed of the enemy thirty-seven, and wounded a great number." Since the Indians as usual carried away their dead, the figure was a guess. All other accounts, however, supported the number as a reasonable estimate.

Kenton and his companion who, like Patten, had seen the Indians' assault, were at Logan's Fort when Patten brought in his grim tidings. They set out to confirm his report and, reaching Boonesborough, happily found that the story was false. A few days later the reinforcements arrived from Virginia.

Now that the immediate Indian danger had passed, suspicions of Boone's activities were again voiced. Colonel Callaway, who had strenuously objected not only to Boone's Paint Creek expedition but also to his willingness to conduct a treaty with Blackfish, preferred formal charges. Both Callaway and Captain Benjamin Logan insisted upon a trial. The court-martial of Daniel Boone was convened at Logan's Fort. The charges were as follows:

i. That Boone had taken out twenty six men to make salt at the Blue Licks, and the Indians had caught him trapping for beaver ten miles below on Licking, and voluntarily surrendered his men at the Licks to the enemy.

ii. That when a prisoner, he engaged with Gov. Hamilton to surrender the people of Boonesborough, to be removed to Detroit, and lived under British protection and jurisdiction.

iii. That returning from captivity, he encouraged a party of men to accompany him to the Paint Lick Town, weakening the garrison at a time when the arrival of an Indian army was daily expected to attack the fort.

iv. That preceding the attack on Boonesborough, he was willing to take the officers of the fort, on pretence of making peace, to the Indian camp, beyond the protection of the guns of the garrison.

Boone defended his actions and loyalty and, after a full investigation, was honorably acquitted on every charge. In fact, he was even promoted to the rank of major for his faithful service. Whether from jealousy, frustration, or some other motive, Callaway and Logan were much displeased with the disposition of the case. Boone's conduct, however, had been fully vindicated.

Daniel soon hurried to North Carolina to see Rebecca and the children. He found them living comfortably at William Bryan's at the Forks of the Yadkin. News of Daniel's escape had come to the settlement, but the story of the defense of Boonesborough, his court-martial, and his promotion was now probably heard for the first time. Very little is known of the Boones' activities from the winter of 1778 through the fall of 1779. They seem to have stayed in the settlements of North Carolina. In the "autobiography" Daniel maintained that "nothing worthy of a place in this account passed in my affairs for some time." But, almost as an afterthought six paragraphs later, he added: "The history of my going home, and returning with my family, forms a series of difficulties, an account of which would swell a volume, and being foreign to my purpose, I shall purposefully omit them."

The reader faced with such a passage can only wonder at the apparent contradiction. It may be, of course, that John Filson received no information from Boone about this period in his life in their interviews and was merely trying to affect a smooth transition in the "autobiography." But if not, what "difficulties"? Why "purposefully omit them"? Boone must have had to make a report to the authorities in Virginia about the present state of affairs in Kentucky. Accurate firsthand information was hard to come by. Were his actions called into doubt again? Some suggested that the "difficulties" had to do with the British sympathies of the Bryan clan, many of whom were Tories. Such a problem may have been one that Boone did not care to pursue. But all statements of this nature are speculative. The fact remained that after a long delay, for whatever reasons, Daniel Boone began to move his family back to Kentucky in October 1779.

7

THE DARK
AND BLOODY
GROUND

MANY CHANGES took place during Daniel's absence from Kentucky. In the spring of 1779 Colonel Bowman mounted an attack on Old Chillicothe with 200 men. He burned the village and destroyed the crops but withdrew without forcing a surrender. During the raid a shot ripped Blackfish's leg open from knee to thigh. Boone's "father" died a few weeks later from the resulting infection.

George Rogers Clark's successful campaign in the summer of 1778 had brought about the capture of the British outposts of Cahokia, Kaskaskia, and Vincennes. Governor Hamilton of Detroit, however, retook Vincennes from Captain Leonard Helm, one of Clark's subordinates, on December 17. It was the first phase of a campaign to be mounted in the spring in which Hamilton hoped to unite all the pro-British tribes, have them meet on the lower Ohio, and, with an estimated 1,000-man force equipped with cannon, drive the Americans back to the seaboard. Clark had to attempt to reconquer Vincennes with only 170 men. He said that if his effort failed, "this country as well as Kentucky I believe is lost."

Clark began his march on February 5, 1779. His attack on February 23 took Hamilton completely by surprise and after two days of fighting and negotiating he was forced to capitulate. Detroit, the cornerstone of the British position in the

West, was a tempting but illogical next target. Clark's men were exhausted and a number of them would have to be left behind to guard their prisoners. That expedition would have to be postponed.

The recapture of Vincennes, combined with other victories by Clark and his officers, had a significant effect upon the war in the West. Dealing from a position of strength that at times was based more on bravado than manpower, they won many Indian tribes away from British influence—the Kaskaskia, Peoria, Chippewa, Ottawa, Potawatomi, Miami, Kickapoo, Wea, Piankeshaw, the more distant Sauk, Fox, Winnebago, and others. They had not broken the British domination of the large tribes, but had raised considerable doubt as to the ultimate success of the British cause in Indians' minds. Indian support became more reluctant and grudging than enthusiastic and willing. Clark's victories also encouraged many new immigrants to the West, most of whom entered Kentucky following Boone's Wilderness Road.

In the fall of 1779 Daniel himself was on the road he had blazed to Boonesborough at the head of his family and a group of new settlers. One of this party is said to have been Abraham Lincoln, the grandfather of the sixteenth president. Since the Boones and Lincolns were longtime friends and related through marriage, the story is a credible one. The first view of Boonesborough may have pleased the Lincolns but could only have disheartened Daniel. In his absence the town he had founded had become a bustling settlement that was too hectic for his liking. The game had retreated and soon so did he. He moved north, near the present town of Athens, to erect Boone's Station on one of his claim sites.

Boone had hurried back to Kentucky to confirm his now invalid Transylvania land claims before the Virginia land commission, which began its hearings in the various forts on October 13. Daniel established a valid title to 1,400 acres for himself and an additional 2,400 acres for his brother George and son Israel. The matter appeared finally to be settled.

The hard winter of 1779–1780 set in around the middle of November. Lured by an exceptionally mild autumn, many immigrants were now snowbound or stopped by drifts in the mountains. As far south as Nashville the rivers were frozen solid. But the weather also kept the speculators away and gave Boone time to sell his land to buy warrants for new tracts. He started for Virginia early in 1780 to purchase the land at "forty pounds for every one hundred acres," the price set by the new law. From his land sales he had raised about twenty thousand dollars, in the depreciated paper currency of the day, and had been given additional money to purchase warrants by Nathaniel Hart and other friends. Daniel had between forty and fifty thousand dollars in cash in his saddlebags when he began his journey. He and his companion got as far as an inn in James City, Virginia, where they stopped, perhaps to get a good night's rest, before entering Williamsburg the next day. They locked the door of their room and placed the saddlebags at the foot of their bed. In the morning they awoke to find the door ajar and the bags gone. Some of the currency was found stuffed in jugs in the cellar of the inn but the vast majority of the sum was never recovered. Boone ever after felt that he was the victim of the landlord of the tavern, though he could prove nothing. The backwoodsmen had probably been drugged to insure a heavy slumber; otherwise their keen hearing would likely have alerted them to the theft.

Boone seems always to have suffered at the hands of civilization. Everything he had struggled to maintain since he first entered Kentucky in 1769 was now gone. In his own words, after the robbery he "was left destitute." Fortune, the wealth he had hoped to derive from the land he was to purchase, was never to be his. He was especially forlorn over the loss of his friends' money. Many held him accountable. Daniel paid them all back, one at a time, over the years. The Hart brothers, who had lost the most, saw the matter differently. In a letter dated August 3, 1780, Thomas Hart summed up their position on the robbery: "I feel for the poor people who perhaps are to loose even their preemptions by it, but I must Say I feel more for poor Boone whose Character I am told Suffers by it." Hart praised Boone as a "Just" and "upright" person, who even in the most "Wretched Sircumstances" was "a Noble and generous Soul." He concluded his comments by stating that "therefore I will freely grant him a discharge for Whatever Sums of mine he might be possest of at the time."

Daniel soon returned to Kentucky, where he had a number of encounters with Indians. While hunting with a large party south of the Kentucky River, he discovered a band of braves advancing toward the camp one night. He quickly directed his men to build a fire and stuff their blankets with beaver pelts to make it appear that the group was asleep. They hid in the brush and waited. At sunrise, a salvo of shots thudded into the bedrolls. The Indians poured into the camp and ran right into the fire of the twenty-five concealed hunters. They beat a hasty retreat back into the forest.

Somewhat later, on a solitary scouting expedition between Boonesborough and the Blue Licks, Boone was fired upon near Slate Creek. He dove into a thicket, crossed the creek, and worked his way downstream to a canebreak. He trained his rifle on the spot where he felt his attacker would appear, but was dismayed when two braves with rifles came stealthily down the creek. He could easily kill one, but in so doing would make himself a perfect target for the second before he could reload. Luck was with him. For an instant the Indians stepped into line in his sights. The shot pierced the lead warrior's head and tore into the other's shoulder. The wounded Indian dropped his gun and ran. Daniel recrossed the creek, took the better rifle, and threw the inferior one into the water before continuing on to the Blue Licks.

Many of the white settlers were not as fortunate as Daniel. One of his relatives, William Bryan, Jr., was killed in March when he went into the woods for his "stray" horse, following the sound of its bell. The Indians had stolen the horse, tied it up, and waited in ambush for the owner. Just before Bryan's death, another of Boone's in-laws met his doom at the hands of the Shawnees. Richard Callaway (Jemima Boone's father-in-law) and Pemberton Rawlings, the two trustees of Boonesborough with whom Daniel had earlier refused to serve, no doubt because of Callaway's charges against him, were unexpectedly attacked only a mile and a half from the fort. Callaway was killed and both were scalped. Rawlings survived but a few hours.

These deaths were a harbinger of the bloodshed yet to come. Major De Peyster, Hamilton's successor as lieutenant-governor of Detroit, planned to make simultaneous attacks on the Spaniards along the Mississippi and the Americans in Kentucky. De Peyster had sent his best agents to buy the Indians' help with amazingly large quantities of weapons. Two of his bills for "Indian goods" from this period totalled in excess of 55,000 pounds.

By June 20 the advance guard of an ever-growing force of 700 Shawnee and Great Lakes Indians had reached Ruddle's Station, one of the northernmost Kentucky settlements. The commander of the expedition, Captain Henry Bird, had marched very slowly from Detroit; he was transporting two cannons and had a detachment of British bombardiers to man them. Against orders his Indian troops fired at the settlers who emerged from Ruddle's Station that same morning, before either piece of artillery had arrived. At noon the small fort was still defensible, but it had just taken two rounds from the newly emplaced light field gun. Then the British six-pounder came up. There was no hope for the station. One or two well-placed shots by the British regulars who manned the heavy cannon would batter down a large section of the stockade. Ruddle's Station was the first fort in Kentucky ever to surrender. Within a week, Martin's Station became the second. The settlers of two other forts, warned of the Indian army's advance, fled. Their homes were burned to the ground.

Bird never had complete control over the Indian forces, especially over those of Great Lakes tribes. With approximately 300 helpless prisoners it was impossible for him to prevent a number of barbarous executions. Probably out of humanitarian motives he refused to continue the expedition and headed his "troops" back to Detroit. The captives became beasts of burden for the Indians, who loaded them down with plunder that often was comprised of the prisoners' own goods.

George Rogers Clark mounted a retaliatory attack on the Shawnees toward the end of July, and was joined by Boone, Logan, and other commanders. Their combined force of about 800 men burned Chillicothe and other villages and committed some atrocities as reprisal for similar acts by the Indians. Starting back to Kentucky on August 9, they were harried by pursuing bands of Indians much of the way.

Boonesborough and its immediate satellite settlements had not been scarred by the Bird campaign. Life seemed reasonably peaceful after the Indian retreat. In October, however, Daniel and his younger brother Edward were returning from a salt-making trip at the Upper Blue Licks and had stopped to graze their horses when a bear suddenly wandered within rifle range. Daniel hurried a shot and followed the animal down the creek while Edward stayed to keep an eye on their horses and equipment and resumed leisurely cracking hickory nuts on some stones. The bear collapsed after running only a short distance and Daniel was about to butcher the carcass when he heard shots ring out from where he had left Edward. Then he heard the baying of a dog that had picked up a scent—his scent. He knew that his brother had been captured or killed and he plunged into a canebrake to try to save himself. He could lose the Indians but not their dog. He had dropped his ramrod and could not reload his rifle, nor could he silence the dog, which easily kept out of his reach. Finally putting some distance between himself and the animal, he grabbed a stalk of cane to serve as a ramrod, loaded, and killed the dog. He then moved off on a new course through the cane, confident that he could now elude the Indians.

Daniel returned to Boonesborough and raised a party to pursue the raiders. The next day they found Edward's decapitated body in the woods. They buried his remains and tracked the retreating braves north as far as the Ohio before giving up the chase.

In November 1780 the Virginia legislature divided Kentucky into Jefferson, Lincoln, and Fayette counties. Jefferson County was located south of the Kentucky River and north and west of the Salt and Green rivers; Lincoln County was south and east of the Salt and Kentucky rivers; and Fayette County was north and east of the Kentucky River. Daniel was soon pressed into service in many roles. He became sheriff, coroner, and county lieutenant of Fayette County, as well as deputy surveyor, lieutenant-colonel of the militia, and a county representative to the Virginia State Assembly.

In April 1781 he was in Richmond for the meeting of the Assembly. The advancing British troops under Cornwallis forced the group to reconvene in Charlottesville, but a detachment under Colonel Banastre Tarleton, a famous Tory partisan, routed the Charlottesville defenders and swarmed into the town with 180 dragoons and 70 mounted infantry. Governor Jefferson and most of the legislators escaped. Daniel and three or four others remained behind to load public records into a wagon. He and John Jouett mounted their horses and slowly made their way toward the edge of town. The British troopers did not challenge the men who, dressed in buckskins, looked like individuals of little consequence. Jouett grew very nervous, however, and addressed Boone as "Colonel" within earshot of a British officer. Both were seized, brought before Tarleton, questioned, and confined.

For some unexplained reason, the two prisoners were paroled after Tarleton rejoined Cornwallis. Perhaps Daniel used the same tactics that he had used to convince Governor Hamilton at Detroit of his loyalty to the British. Or perhaps one of Rebecca's Tory relatives, who was said to have been in Tarleton's detachment, arranged his release. One story said that he escaped. What actually happened has never been ascertained.

Daniel was still a prisoner on June 17 and was released too late to finish the legislative session, which ended on June 23 in Staunton. By the end of August he was back in Kentucky to meet his new son Nathan, who was to be his last child. In November he returned to Virginia for the next legislative session, which lasted until January 1782, after which he again returned to Kentucky.

Although in the East, Cornwallis had been forced to surrender in October 1781, neither the Americans nor the British were willing to accept the stalemate that existed in the West. From 1780 on, both sides had suffered from a lack of trained troops, insufficient provisions and armament, and a rugged terrain that forestalled decisive victory or defeat. The frontier had some of its bitterest fighting still ahead of it. Kentucky was to suffer such an increase of fearsome Indian attacks that 1782 was justly called its "year of blood."

News of Cornwallis's defeat did not reach Detroit until April 13 and throughout the winter, the British authorities prepared to launch another invasion into Kentucky. The raids began as early as February. To make matters worse, the savage Wyandots, who had now made peace with the more eastern tribes, joined the British cause. In March a band of twenty-five Wyandot warriors passed by Boonesborough without incident, but caught a young girl and a black man outside the stockade of Estill's Station. They killed her within full view of the fort and carried him off as a prisoner. Captain Estill and his twenty-five-man garrison were away at that time on a scouting mission, but two months later Estill led a party of about eighteen of his men in pursuit of an Indian band, probably the same Wyandots. A savage two-hour battle ensued when the twenty-five warriors were overtaken. Apparently seventeen Indians were killed and two wounded; only three whites survived. In June the Indians decisively defeated a force of approximately 500 militia from Virginia and Pennsylvania on the Sandusky River in Ohio. Colonel William Crawford, the commander, died only after a two-hour ordeal of slowly burning at the stake, during which he was scalped and had burning coals poured on his bleeding head. Simon Girty, the much feared "white Indian," watched the spectacle with great enjoyment.

August marked the high point of the Indian onslaught. Seventy braves attacked Hoy's Station in what is now Madison County, captured two boys, and started north toward the Ohio at a sluggish pace. It was a diversionary raid meant to draw the white forces away from Bryan's Station, the object of the main attack, and it almost worked. Captain Holder gathered up what men he could at Hoy's, sent messages to all the other stations to send men, and rushed after the Indians. When he received the news, Boone put others in command at his station and hurried to Boonesborough to raise a party. Bryan's Station was the scene of similar activity. Meanwhile, Holder had ridden into a trap in which many of his men were wounded, some mortally. They were forced to retreat without even catching a glimpse of the prisoners they had hoped to rescue.

Before the main force of over 300 Indians left Chillicothe, they were stirred by the following now famous speech of Simon Girty:

Brothers: The fertile region of Kentucky is the land of cane and clover—spontaneously growing to feed the buffalo, the elk and the deer. There the bear and the beaver are always fat. The Indians from all the tribes have had a right from time immemorial, to hunt and kill unmolested these wild animals, and bring off their skins—to purchase for themselves clothing, to buy blankets for their backs and rum to send down their throats, to drive away the cold and rejoice their hearts after the fatigues of hunting and the toil of war. [Great applause.]

Brothers, the long knives [i.e., Virginians] have overrun your country and usurped your hunting grounds. They have destroyed the cane, trodden down the clover, killed the deer and the buffalo, the beaver and the raccoon. The beaver has been chased from his dam, and forced to leave the country. [Palpable emotion among the hearers.]

Brothers: The intruders on your land exult in the success that has crowned their flagitious acts. They are planting fruit trees and plowing the lands where, not long since, were the canebrake and the clover field. Was there a voice in the tree of forest, or articulate sounds in the gurgling waters, every part of this country would call on you to chase away these ruthless invaders, who are laying it waste. Unless you rise in the majesty of your might and exterminate their whole race, you may bid adieu to the hunting grounds of your fathers—to the delicious flesh of the animals with which they once abounded—and to the skins with which you were once enabled to purchase your clothing and your rum.

Excise the rhetoric of war from Girty's words and what remains is a remarkably fair statement of the Indians' point of view and an eloquent expression of a valid complaint. The renegade white, who was regarded as the scourge of the frontier by the settlers, knew that the clash between Indians and whites was inherent in their opposing views of the function and use of the wilderness. Girty did much to agitate the tribes to make war on the intruders, perhaps because he recognized that conflict between these two cultures was inevitable.

Spurred on by Girty's speech, the Indians, under the command of British officers—William Caldwell, Alexander McKee, and Matthew Elliott—and of Simon and George Girty, secretly surrounded Bryan's Station on August 15 or 16. By sheer luck the men inside the fort were still preparing to march off to the aid of Hoy's Station. The war party would not have the easy prey it expected. No one knows how the settlers discovered the Indian presence. One unverified story stated that a messenger brought word of the attack just before the Indians' arrival. In any event, the gates stood closed and the men manned the bastions. The settlers had had no time to bring in the cattle or collect water and knew that they could not long withstand a siege under the hot August sun. The Indians, for their part, were unsure of the situation they were facing. Was the fort essentially undefended, its men having gone off to the relief of Hoy's Station, or was the twelve-foot-high stockade occupied by forty-four expert shots? They waited. Before dawn a black was attacked and an Indian scout killed. Girty and Caldwell, the main Indian commanders, hoped the settlers would imagine that the dead brave was part of a small raiding party, and continued to wait in ambush for the men of the fort. They were so intent on not revealing their position and number that they let two messengers from the station slip unmolested through their lines.

Within the fort it was decided that the women would have to go to the spring to get water. It was their normal chore and if the daily routine was carried out perhaps the Indians would not fire. Hopefully the war party would believe itself still undetected and wait to ambush the men who would soon leave the stockade. There would be no favoritism—all the females in the fort would go. They knelt in prayer, then picked up their buckets and other containers and walked casually to the spring at intervals. They valiantly kept up cheerful talk in the groups, gathered all the water they could, and, trembling inwardly, began the seemingly endless walk back to the stockade. Once they were safe inside the fort the gates were quickly shut and barred. Thanks to the women, the garrison now had a chance to repel the impending assault.

As the morning grew late and the gates remained closed, Girty became impatient. He ordered a small attack on the wall furthest away from the main body of his troops as a decoy. It was an old trick and one the men of Bryan's Station were familiar with. They had an equally small party make a great show of flinging open cabin doors, firing, and running after the Indians. Most of the men stood at the loopholes in the stockade with their rifles cocked. Girty thought his plan had worked and ordered the principal attack. By this time the pursuing band of whites had gotten nearly back to the stockade; they soon brought the garrison up to full strength. The men had two or three rifles each and the women kept them loaded. The deadly marksmanship of the frontiersmen soon forced the Indians to give up the attack and take cover.

Girty, a formidable tactician, knew he had little chance of taking the fort before the messengers brought help, and prepared to ambush the relief columns instead. The messengers had overtaken Major Levi Todd and his thirty riflemen at Boone's Station, where Captain William Ellis was in command of sixteen or seventeen mounted men. Both forces rushed to the aid of Bryan's Station. As they approached all was quiet, too quiet. The commanders recognized the ambush. They decided that Ellis's cavalry would ride straight through the trap at full speed to try to reach the station and that the foot soldiers would try to get to the compound using the nearby cover of a hundred acres of tall corn. Tradition holds that the dust raised by the galloping horses prevented the Indians from getting a clear shot. All of the horsemen reached the fort. The men on foot were less fortunate—the cornfield also provided the Indians with excellent cover. The men in the fort heard the sounds of the battle gradually fading away, as their would-be rescuers fled back to Lexington, leaving two dead comrades behind.

Girty realized that his men probably could not take a fort defended by some sixty rifles. He decided to try guile. He yelled out a demand that the garrison surrender, saying he had cannons which would arrive by evening. If they gave up now, they would not be harmed. If they chose to fight, his artillery would smash down the stockade and no quarter would be given. For a moment the settlers, no doubt remembering the fate of Ruddle's and Martin's stations, were silent. Then Aaron Reynolds, reputed to be one of the mightiest of frontier cursers, showered Girty with a volley of insults that broke the tension. There would be no surrender. A few random shots directed at the fort kept the defenders at their posts all night, but by daybreak the Indians were gone.

Reinforcements arrived the next day. The scene that greeted them could only inspire an avenging anger. Everything outside the fort that would burn had been reduced to rubble. All the animals had been killed and the crops destroyed. By noon the men of Bryan's Station, together with the troops from Boonesborough, Harrodsburg, and Lexington, the total force numbering less than two hundred, sallied forth on the trail of the Indians. The commanders had decided not to wait for the four or five hundred additional men coming up from the south under Colonel Benjamin Logan. Boone was in charge of one of the divisions, which contained his son Israel and numerous other relations. John Todd and Stephen Trigg commanded the other divisions.

The Indian force had retreated in one group, an unusual maneuver that made their trail impossible to miss. The Kentuckians moved swiftly through the wilderness after the war party, covering over thirty miles in twelve hours. Coming upon the Indians' camp of the previous night, Boone counted the fires and revised the estimate of their enemies' strength to "at least 500 Indians." Daniel grew more suspicious with each step he took. The Indians were making no attempt to disguise their tracks; in fact, they had blazed trees with their tomahawks.

By the following morning the whites had made their way to the Licking River near the Lower Blue Licks ford. The scouts could find only two Indians on a ridge ahead of them. Todd, the senior officer in command, asked for Boone's advice. Daniel said that the signs he read, of Indians stepping in each others' tracks to conceal their numbers, indicated an ambush. He proposed crossing further upriver to avoid this possibility, but was overruled. After sighting a few Indians on a hill a mile away, Todd again called upon Daniel's judgment. Boone urged that they wait for Logan and his troops. Even after the scouts returned with the report that all was clear for more than a mile ahead, Boone asserted that the two ravines which connected the hill with the river could easily hide the entire Indian force. Todd seemed inclined to heed Boone's warning. Unfortunately Hugh McGary, still smarting from a remark made about his courage when he suggested waiting for Logan at Bryan's Station two days before, was determined to prove himself. He thrust his rifle over his head and spurred his horse into the river, screaming: "All who are not damned cowards follow me, and I'll soon show you the Indians."

The three commanders watched helplessly as their men followed McGary's lead. They managed to regroup the enthusiastic mob on the opposite shore into three columns. The whites left most of their horses at the river and crested the ridge on foot.

The advance guard of twenty-five men, which included Boone, Todd, Trigg, and McGary, moved down the hill and toward the ravines. As they got within about sixty yards of the suspect ravines, they were caught in a murderous volley. Twenty-two were killed. Boone, McGary, and one other survived. In the next three minutes eighteen more were dead. Boone rejoined his column and managed to drive the enemy momentarily back. But the other two columns, now without their leaders, had given way. The Kentuckians ran panic-stricken back toward the river—with a few exceptions, it was every man for himself. The actual battle lasted only five minutes. Boone tried to keep his men together and escape to the west into the forest. A rifle ball whistled past him. He spun around to see blood pouring from his son's mouth. Daniel was so intent on saving Israel that he let a Wyandot brave get within a few feet of him before he could put his son down and fire. He saw that Israel was dead or dying and left him on the ground. He and most of his men were able to recross the Licking at a ford near the mouth of Indian Creek.

Many others were not so fortunate. When the Indians saw the settlers break and run they discarded their rifles for tomahawks and scalping knives. They reached the horses left by the riverbank at the same time as the whites and wreaked destruction and havoc on all sides. An act of cool courage by a man named Benjamin Netherland saved a number of Kentuckians from the ranks of the massacred. Netherland rode his horse across the Licking and could have easily continued on to complete safety. Seeing the slaughter occurring on the opposite bank, he dismounted and organized the men fleeing by him into a line. On his command, ten to twenty rifles were fired, and the Indians, many of whom had no rifles, were forced to retreat. Netherland thus gained precious minutes for a number of his comrades to cross the river and escape the scalping knife.

On Monday, August 19, the day of the battle, Colonel Logan and his troops arrived at Bryan's Station only to find that Todd had proceeded without him. He started after them immediately but within a few miles met the first of the fleeing Blue Licks survivors. He prepared to repel the attack by the braves, whom he felt must be right on the heels of the terrified settlers. The trickle of survivors continued through the night and then stopped. There was no attack.

The Indians were meanwhile taking scalps and literally evening the score. They counted sixty white scalps and sixty-four dead braves, then killed four of their prisoners. In the "autobiography" Boone stated the simple horror of the Blue

Licks defeat: "Many widows were now made." Over one-third of the expedition was killed. Nearly every home suffered a loss.

Logan moved his men up to the Licking but refused to cross, rightly suspecting a second ambush. On August 24, Boone joined Logan's larger force on a second march to the Blue Licks, after he had returned from breaking the news to Rebecca at Boone's Station. The aftermath of the massacre was an almost unbearable sight to behold. Some of the slashed, disfigured corpses still had their hands tied. These were the unfortunates taken alive by the Wyandots. The five days of heat had bloated the mangled bodies, which could often be distinguished from each other only by remnants of clothing not stripped away by the Indians, wolves, and vultures. They buried the bodies they could find in a common grave. Boone found Israel's body and brought it back to his station for burial.

Recriminations over responsibility for the Blue Licks disaster occupied over a month's time. Logan blamed George Rogers Clark for calling away a hundred men to defend Louisville and western Kentucky and thus weakening the local militia. Clark stated that the defeat was a direct result of the officers in charge: "The conduct of those unfortunate Gents was extremely reprehensible." Boone was never named as one of the parties at fault by either side, but was deeply disturbed by his inability to convince the others of the ambush ahead of them. He felt responsible for the bloody defeat.

The dispute finally abated. In the fall, Clark led a force of 1,000 riflemen against the Indian towns. Benjamin Logan and John Floyd served as his seconds in command, and Boone headed his own detachment. They burned Chillicothe for the third time, laid waste to the village of Piqua on the Miami River, and destroyed all the crops they could find. The expedition encountered little resistance.

Blue Licks was the last major battle of the Revolutionary War. Preliminary peace talks opened between the Americans and the British in November 1782. But Indian raids, though much reduced, continued well after the signing of the formal treaty on April 19, 1783. The British stopped supplying the

Indians with weapons, but found it far more difficult to halt attacks than it had been to inspire them. Immigrants moving down the Ohio on flatboats, hunters and trappers in the woods, and settlers whose farms were remote from the forts, all were victims of sporadic Indian raids until General "Mad Anthony" Wayne finally defeated the Indians at Fallen Timbers in 1794.

About the same time as the 1783 Treaty of Paris, which brought the Revolutionary War to a close, Daniel Boone had one of his closest escapes. He had taken to raising some tobacco as a cash crop to supplement his income and had built a small curing shed. One day when he was on the poles or rafters of the shed raising a tier of dried leaves to add more tobacco below, he looked down and discovered four grinning Shawnees. One of them said, "Now, Boone, we got you. You no get away any more. We carry you off to Chillicothe this time. You no cheat us any more." Daniel was in no position to disagree. He was suspended in the air, far from his cabin, and unarmed. He struck up a pleasant conversation to gain time and assured the warriors he would enjoy going back to Chillicothe to see his old friends. All the while he was gathering rows of dried tobacco in his hands. He explained that he wanted to finish his work and told them to watch him closely. In an instant he dumped all the tobacco and tobacco dust in their faces, jumped down pulling as much more tobacco upon them as he could, and ran for his house. Looking back from a distance, he could not resist a chuckle. The braves were still stumbling around rubbing their eyes, and all the while swearing at Boone for having tricked them again.

8

LAND TROUBLE AND
ON TO MISSOURI

SOMETIME PROBABLY IN 1783 Daniel Boone moved his family to Limestone, Kentucky. The town served as an outfitting station and jumping-off point for Kentucky immigrants coming down the Ohio River. It was a perfect spot for trading, general business, and land speculation. Daniel meant to do the best he could at all three. He opened a store and tavern and functioned as a surveyor.

By the end of 1783 he was a deputy surveyor in both Lincoln and Fayette counties and, because of his reputation as an explorer, drew more than his share of work. It has been calculated that Daniel completed almost 150 surveys of claims in the next three years. Surveying was a lucrative but dangerous business. Daniel did a great deal of work for absentee claimants who entrusted him with treasury warrants to purchase land. He received up to half of the land he surveyed for them in return for finding good land and guaranteeing a free and clear title to it. The danger in the enterprise came not from the Indians, who still kept up fairly active raids. He knew their ways and could defend himself against them. The danger came from his guaranteeing his clients a clear legal title to the lands he laid out and purchased in their names. He was a tolerable surveyor and better than most in the inclusion of landmarks. But the surveys of the period were rough at best and warrants had been issued for more land than existed. Boone's haphazard technique was illustrated in a survey made for himself, dated "Aperel the 22 1785," for a claim on the Kentucky River: "Survayd for Dal Boone 5000 acres begin at Robert Camels NE Corner at at [sic] 2 White ashes and Buckeyes S 1200 p[oles] to 3 Shuger trees Ealm and walnut E 666 p to 6 Shuger trees and ash N 1200 p to a poplar and beech W 666 p to the begining." Conflict was inevitable.

More often than not Boone failed to complete the legal steps necessary to insure ownership of land. The worst trouble was with his own claims. He seems to have entered into the surveying business with such relish that he did not take the time to work through the lengthy process of land registration. He never thought anyone would question the legality of his claims. He was wrong. Not all of his land was lost through cross-filings and eventual suits of ejectment, however. Boone frequently sold what he believed to be his land, in good faith, to raise money for further speculation. When his buyers found that he had unknowingly sold them land to which other claimants held the valid title, they sued him for damages, and what land he truly owned he had to sell to repay his debts. Not until his last years was he finally able to state that he owed money to no man.

Daniel fared better as a tavern proprietor and businessman. He carried on a lively trade not only with the many settlers on the move to the interior of Kentucky, but also with the government. He supplied the needs of the Indian prisoners taken in the area. One of his first bills sent to the state of Virginia, dated October 15, 1786, indicated the cordial treatment that the Indians received. Boone asked payment of three pounds for the "19 galons of Whiskey Delivered to the Indins priseners on there first arrivel at Limeston." By mid-1787 he was doing such a volume of business in feeding the captured Indians that he made up a special account ledger which he entitled "Daniel Boones Indan Book."

The Indians also were active in taking prisoners. For the period from 1783 to 1790, estimates ran as high as 1,500 Kentucky settlers either captured or killed. Starting in 1784, Boone wrote a telling contingency clause into his contractual agreements: "I will Bee accountable for any money put into his hands inless kild by Indians." In a letter written late in the summer of 1785, Daniel reported the killing of two men at Squire Boone's settlement and flatly stated that "in Short an Inden Warr is Exspcted." The war never materialized but the harassing raids continued. One of the largest took place on May 23, 1786, when a party of 200 warriors attacked flatboats on the Ohio near its confluence with the Kentucky River.

George Rogers Clark and Benjamin Logan each headed a column in a retaliatory attack against the Indians. Clark's targets were the tribes along the Wabash, while Logan, accompanied by Boone, directed his force against the Shawnee towns on the Miami. Part of the mission was to take prisoners to exchange for white captives. Late on the night of September 29 and into the wee hours of the following day, Logan's troops crossed the river. They took the Indians by surprise, many of the braves having already left to fight Clark. Boone recognized a familiar face in a band of fleeing Shawnees and told his companions to beware of that warrior. It was Big Jim, Boone's "friend," who thirteen years earlier had tortured his eldest son James to death in Powell's Valley. As the white pursuers closed the gap, Big Jim turned and fired, killing one man and killing or wounding another before he himself was killed. About nineteen other warriors fell victim to the settlers' rifles and over seventy prisoners were taken. The old chief Moluntha and his squaw were among those who surrendered.

Moluntha appeared not to fear capture, and with good reason. He had been working with American officials for some time, trying to free or exchange captive whites. At the white camp the chief was soon confronted by Major Hugh McGary, who for four years had been labeled as the man responsible for the Blue Licks massacre. McGary demanded to know if Moluntha remembered the battle. The chief, who in all likelihood did not understand the question and had not been present at

Blue Licks, answered yes, he did recall it. The irrational McGary cursed Moluntha and split his head open with two quick blows of a small ax. Before he could be restrained, he turned his vengeance on Moluntha's wife, cutting off three of her fingers with the next swipe of his ax. Although Boone and others were outraged at this senseless act, McGary's punishment was less than severe. He was reprimanded and stripped of his commission by a court-martial.

The prisoner exchange sometimes moved too slowly to suit Daniel Boone. At one point he rescued a small girl named Chloe Flinn from the Indians and cared for her for over a year before locating her family. In March 1787 the Indians released a boy upon Boone's word that one of their braves would also be freed. Boone probably saved the boy from months of captivity by his abuse of official procedures. When upbraided for his conduct by an officer, Daniel angrily wrote, "I am hire With my hands full of Bisness and No athority and if I am Not indulged in What I Do for the best it Is Not worth my While to put my Self to all this trubel." No more was said of the matter.

Preliminary peace negotiations began in April 1787 with the return of four white prisoners as a token of good faith. Nine captives were exchanged late in the same month. Boone fed them all, white and red. On August 20, the new Indian leaders—Captain Johnny, Wolf, and others—met with Boone, Logan, Levi Todd, Kenton, and a few more white diplomats at Limestone (now renamed Maysville) and successfully drew up a formal treaty. After the all-night celebration feast, Boone's son Daniel Morgan Boone went hunting with the Shawnee chief Blue Jacket as a symbol of the new peace. The treaty proved to be less than effective. The Indians who signed the agreement represented only five of the villages within striking distance of Maysville. Those groups who had not signed the document continued to send out war parties.

Even the inhabitants of the friendly villages sometimes broke the peace. Blue Jacket, the friend of Daniel's son, was to cause the elder Boone a great deal of embarrassment. In the spring of 1788, Blue Jacket was apprehended after stealing eight to ten horses from Strode's Station. He was brought to

Maysville, which had made Boone and Kenton two of its trustees the preceding year, and was put in Daniel's custody. Boone had recently come back to Kentucky after a trip to Pennsylvania with his wife and son Nathan to visit his family. This was not the type of homecoming welcome he appreciated. Daniel did the only thing he could. He regretfully had the chief bound and locked in the sturdiest cabin in the settlement to await trial. But someone, no one knew who, either left a knife sticking in one of the logs of the cabin or put it there deliberately. With it, Blue Jacket managed to cut his bonds and escape. Boone was the object of a number of suspicious sideways glances.

By this time Daniel Boone had become famous. The "autobiography" of the pioneer, "The Adventures of Col. *Daniel Boon . . .* " had been published in 1784 as a thirty-four page appendix to John Filson's *The Discovery, Settlement And present State of Kentucke*. Filson's work was not a financial success, but it brought Boone international prominence. The work was translated and reprinted in France and Germany within a year of its publication. By 1785 the "Adventures" had been extracted from Filson's book and printed in America in an edited form in which many of Filson's overly ornamented oratorical phrases and passages were deleted. In the new edition Daniel's portrayal as a somewhat verbose eighteenth-century philosopher who could ironically wax eloquent over both the beauties of nature and the joys of civilization was deemphasized. He was now characterized as more of a hunter, explorer, and Indian fighter. His story was, in fact, made more appealing to the average American citizen—the pace of the "autobiography" was quickened and the reader's attention was focused upon action rather than words.

Daniel also enjoyed a newfound affluence. He was now one of the wealthiest men in Kentucky. During his residence at Maysville he had purchased three slaves. Legal suits against him proceeded slowly and had not made any substantial dent in the nearly 100,000 acres of land he had under claim. It was the most prosperous period in his life.

Why, then, did he move to Point Pleasant in Kanawha

County, Virginia, sometime in 1789 or 1790? Perhaps it was his old case of the "itching foot" flaring up again. He certainly was on the move. In May 1789 Daniel was on the Monongahela with a drove of horses for sale. Two months later he wrote to a business client that he expected to be in Philadelphia that winter. In October the Kanawha residents recognized his talents in a popular petition which asked that he be appointed lieutenant-colonel of the county militia. The petition was quickly recommended for approval by the county court, but the official commission did not arrive until April 1791.

A description of how Boone, now in his mid-fifties, appeared to one of his new Kanawha neighbors yielded a pleasing picture of the man: "His large head, full chest, square shoulders, and stout form are still impressed upon my mind. He was (I think) about five feet ten inches in height, and his weight say 175. He was solid in mind as well as in body, never frivolous, thoughtless, or agitated; but was always quiet, meditative, and impressive, unpretentious, kind, and friendly in his manner."

Boone seems to have been a silent delegate to the 1791 Virginia Assembly. Although he served on two committees, one on religion and the other on propositions and licenses, he evidently did little more than vote. He did, however, give guidance for the defense of the county through the proper allocation of military personnel—the "Privets" and "sypes or scutes" (spies or scouts). Still the businessman, on December 13, 1791, Daniel offered to take ammunition to Redstone in return for the contract to supply provisions to his county's militia. While in Richmond he phrased the matter this way in a letter to the governor:

Sir as sum purson Must Carry out the armantstion [ammunition] to Red Stone [Brownsville, Pa.] if your Exelency Should have thought me a proper purson I Would undertake it on Condistions I have the apintment to vitel the Company at Kanhowway So that I Could take Down the Flower as I paste the place. I am your Excelency most obedent omble Sarvent,

Dal Boone

Five days later the contract was awarded to him. Receipts which have survived testify to his delivery of lead, flints, and powder to various military outposts.

Daniel Boone proved to be less than successful as a supply officer, however. In 1792 and 1793 Captain Hugh Caperton and Colonel William Clendenin complained in writing that on one occasion Boone refused to deliver provisions and that on another he agreed to delivery but neither he nor the consignment ever arrived. Boone likely had a running verbal battle with Caperton, and since Daniel was a man of few words, in one instance he just grabbed his rifle and left camp for a number of days. Questioned about his actions, he would only say that "Caperton did not do to my liken." Others must have echoed his sentiments for Caperton soon went before a court-martial and was relieved of his command.

In 1785 Boone had begun to face enemies he was ill-equipped to fight—lawyers. The suits of ejectment trickled in at first, but by 1798 the constant barrage had left him essentially landless. The fearless Shel-tow-ee found that he was rendered helpless by a confusing jumble of legal jargon and technicalities. Some of his early losses are easily explained. He was a guileless man bilked by smooth-talking con artists. He once secured a 500-pound bond for one Ebenezer Platt and loaned the man a horse and equipment for a trip to Louisville. It turned out that Platt had been an inmate at Newgate Prison in England. His route to Louisville was less than direct, his next known whereabouts being New Orleans. Boone never seemed able to realize that treating a man honestly did not guarantee being treated honestly in return. He took a 1,000-pound bond for land from Gilbert Imlay, who was later to sail for England and become the lover of Mary Wollstonecraft, the mother of Mary Shelley. Before his departure Imlay sold the land he had never paid for and in 1786 wrote Boone an apologetic note claiming he could not redeem the debt.

Boone was not alone in his losses. Imagine the reaction of the inhabitants of Bryan's Station, who, after having survived both a siege and the battle of Blue Licks, were confronted in

1784 with a Virginian who was now the legal owner of the station. It was the first time that he had been in Kentucky.

Daniel was understandably embittered by his experiences. Not only did he lose his land and become submerged in debt through lawsuits, but he fell from public esteem. The honored pioneer became perhaps the most hated man in Kentucky. Because of his vast knowledge of the land and his great activity in surveying, he was often an "expert" witness in the countless lawsuits over "shingled" claims in which he had no other involvement. Each case had to have a loser, a party who felt cheated. Boone made so many enemies that even his honesty was impugned. He was called a liar and accused of being a "chimney corner" surveyor, one who sat by his chimney and set down property boundaries from memory, or worse, from imagination.

Daniel decided to distance himself as much as he could from the machinery of the law and vowed never to defend any suit against land he had under claim. He gave the one tract of land he possessed which had not been cross-filed to his nephew, Colonel John Grant, with instructions to use it to repay anyone with a valid claim against him. By 1795—the year in which General "Mad Anthony" Wayne finally forced the Indians in the Northwest Territory to sign the Treaty of Greenville, after their defeat at Fallen Timbers—Boone had resettled his family at Brushy Fork near the Blue Licks. He hunted and farmed for the next few years even though game was scarce and rheumatism at times made the simplest task an ordeal.

Early in 1796, Daniel heard that the Wilderness Road was to be widened to accommodate travel by wagons. Kentucky had become the fifteenth state in 1792 and Isaac Shelby, an old acquaintance from the Boonesborough days during the Revolution, was its first governor. As Daniel put pen to paper on February 11, 1796, he had hopes of recouping some of his losses. The letter to Shelby read as follows:

Sir—After my best Respts to your Excelancy and family I wish to inform you that I have sum intention of undertaking this New Rode

114

that is to be cut through the Wilderness and I think my Self intitled to
the ofer of the Bisness as I first Marked out that Rode in March 1775
and Never rec'd anything for my trubel and Sepose I am no States-
man I am a Woodsman and think My Self as Capable of Marking and
Cutting that Rode, as any other man Sir if you think with Me I would
thank you to wright me a Line by the post the first oportuneaty and
he will lodge it at Mr. John Milers on Hinkston fork as I wish to know
Wheer and when it is to be Latt [let] So that I may attend at the time
I am Deer Sir

> *your very omble servent*
> *Daniel Boone*

Shelby's reply either did not survive or was never made. In any case, Daniel Boone was not given the opportunity of "Cutting that Rode." That fall he went on a bear hunt up the Big Sandy River and stayed until spring.

Although sixty-two and rheumatic, Daniel Boone kept faith in his dream of owning land where the game was plentiful. His dream, essentially the same dream his grandfather George had when he left England for Pennsylvania, also passed on to his children. Again like his grandfather, Daniel sent his son Daniel Morgan Boone ahead to investigate the possibilities of a new "promised land"—Missouri. Young Daniel hunted and explored the region along the Mississippi between 1795 and 1797 and met Don Zenon Trudeau, the Spanish lieutenant-governor. Trudeau wished to encourage settlement, and knowing full well that where Daniel Boone went many others would eagerly follow, promised handsome grants of land to the old pioneer and those who accompanied him. Young Boone hurried back to Kentucky to explain the proposition to his father and to describe the region's abundant game and fertile soil. He returned to Missouri in 1798 and made one more trip back to Kentucky the following year to confer with his father. Daniel Morgan Boone had already settled in St. Charles County, Missouri.

The elder Daniel had grown cautious with age. All of his best land was gone, but in 1797 he still held title to over 27,000 acres of second- and third-rate land. The irony of two occurrences in 1798 may have helped him to make the decision to migrate. That year, when a county of Kentucky was named in his honor, the sheriffs of Mason and Clark counties sold over 10,000 acres of his land for back taxes.

Boone left Kentucky in September 1799. His contemporary, George Washington, died later that same year, but Boone, two months shy of his sixty-fifth birthday, was again pulling up stakes and moving west. James Fenimore Cooper used this event to forge another link between Boone and the main character of his Leatherstocking Tales. At the beginning of *The Prairie*, the author describes a "resolute forester" who migrated to Missouri in later life. In a footnote, Cooper identifies the figure as "Colonel Boon, the patriarch of Kentucky," who at the close of the eighteenth century emigrated for much the same reasons as Leatherstocking. Boone left "because he found a population of ten to the square mile, inconveniently crowded."

The real Boone took a bit more of civilization with him than Cooper's spartan Leatherstocking. He fashioned a sixty-foot dugout canoe out of a huge tulip poplar to carry most of the family and household goods, and drove their stock along the overland route himself, perhaps accompanied by Jemima's husband, Flanders Callaway. As Trudeau had anticipated, a good number of Boone's friends and relatives decided to go to Missouri with him.

Legend has it that it was on this journey that Daniel, while stopped at Cincinnati, was asked why he was leaving Kentucky. "Too many people!" was the famous reply. "Too crowded! too crowded! I want more elbow-room."

Boone and his party reached St. Louis by October 1799. The bedraggled pioneer was welcomed with full military honors by both Trudeau and his successor as lieutenant-governor, Carlos D. Delassus. Trudeau had stressed to Delassus the importance of keeping the agreements made with Boone. Delassus agreed and went so far as to put Daniel in charge both of portioning out the land grants to his followers and of selecting the site of each parcel.

Daniel directed the operation mainly from the home of his son Daniel Morgan in the Femme Osage district sixty miles west of St. Louis. Each settler received from four hundred to six hundred arpents of land with an additional forty arpents for each family member or servant. (Each arpent was the equivalent of .85 acre.) Boone, as the leader of the settlers, was rewarded with one thousand arpents anywhere in the district. He had quite a choice before him. The Femme Osage comprised everything north of the Missouri River and had no given western boundary. The tract which he selected was mostly bottomland that abutted his son's estate upon the north. Daniel erected a small log cabin but, perhaps for convenience, made the mistake of constructing it on his son's property. By February 1800, Daniel and Rebecca had built a sugar camp on the land of their other son, Nathan, and produced some 300–400 pounds of maple sugar over a period of some weeks.

Soon Daniel led his family into a new land scheme. On the banks of the Missouri River about five miles below the present town of Augusta, they plotted out a settlement called Missouriton, or "Daniel Boone's Palatinate," and hoped to attract wealthy Virginians as citizens. The town prospered briefly but a large part of its surveyed land was eventually carried away by a shift in the course of the river. Daniel consoled himself with the excellent prospects of trapping and hunting.

Meanwhile, on July 11, 1800, he was made the "syndic," or magistrate, of Femme Osage by Lieutenant-Governor Delassus. Daniel already exerted much power, for he had continued to serve as the disburser of land to all new settlers. Now he was also the judge, jury, sheriff, and commandant of the district. In effect he was the *patron* or Spanish *don* of the territory. As the Lewis and Clark expedition proceeded up the Missouri, Meriwether Lewis noted Boone's influence on the people in and around St. Charles, stating that they "yeald passive obedience to the will of their temporal master, the Commandant." Although the Louisiana Territory passed from Spanish to French hands in October 1800, it never drew any attention from the French authorities. Spain and her officers, such as Daniel Boone, continued to govern.

Despite his many obligations as syndic, Daniel managed to indulge his favorite endeavor—hunting. His first few trips were for enjoyment, but the ventures could be commercially profitable as well. Markets in St. Louis paid forty cents per pound for deerskins and did not demand that the hides be grained. Not having to scrape off the hair gave the riflemen additional time to hunt and increased the weight of their skins. Daniel joined his sons in commercial hunting sometime late in the summer of 1801.

The winter trapping season was a disaster for Boone. One of his beaver traps snapped shut on his hand and he had to go back to camp for help to open the steel jaws. The camp was later robbed by the Indians of the little it held. Daniel finished the season with only thirty or forty pelts to his credit, which his son Nathan used to pay part of the Kentucky debts. As a final blow, his rheumatism flared up for the next few winters and eliminated any trapping activity.

This bad luck and illness did not dampen Boone's spirit. He enjoyed his first years in Missouri more than any other time since his first hunt in Kentucky more than thirty years earlier. He and his fellow settlers adjusted well to their new life under Spanish rule. A problem might have developed over religion, since each new immigrant technically had to be a Catholic. While public policy was stringently adhered to, Trudeau and Delassus kept their word that any religion might be practiced in private. Each incoming settler faced questions to determine his or her religion that almost all Christians, whether they were Catholic or not, could answer in the affirmative. After listening to the expected replies to such queries as "Do you believe in God Almighty?" the examiners proclaimed each Baptist or Methodist a good Catholic. Similar lenience marked the official behavior towards visiting Protestant preachers. No notice was taken of them until their tour of ministry was nearly complete. Then a warning was delivered demanding that they leave the district in three days or be arrested. All complied, only to return on the next tour and be ordered out of the country again when they were ready to leave. Matters went so well with the new immigrants in the next few years that the Spanish authorities offered Boone ten thousand arpents if he would induce a hundred additional American families to settle west of the Mississippi. Boone's name still exerted a magic drawing power upon pioneers. The people came and Daniel got his land.

In his role as syndic, Boone held court near his cabin under what came to be known as the "Justice Tree." Not unexpectedly, this court was very different from any court that Boone had ever encountered. He was the judge and jury and even supervised the implementation of the sentence—usually a whipping with the strokes "well laid on." A guilty offender could be tried, sentenced, punished, and released into society as a reputable citizen, all within an hour or two. The court reflected its magistrate; it was honest, fearless, and straight from the shoulder. Daniel observed no rules of evidence, saying that he only wished to know the truth. If his justice was less than subtle, it was often a good match for the crime. Some surviving legal documents show that the district over which he ruled was far from peaceful:

June 30th, 1804
This Day Came before me Justice of the Peace for the District of the Femmosage, Francis Woods, Peter Smith & John Manley and made oath that on the 29th of June of said Month at the house of David Bryan a Certain James Meek and the Bearer hereof Bery Vinzant had some differance Which Came to blows and in the scuffle the said James Meek bit of[f] a piece of Bery Vinzants Left Ear, further the Deponent sayeth not[.] Given under my hand and seal the day and Date above written

Daniel Boone [Seal]

Those who appeared before Boone's bench did not object to his rough-and-ready approach. When one offender whom Daniel had sentenced to a number of lashes was asked how he fared, the reply was: "First rate. Whipped and cleared." Boone's contemporaries stated that the old frontiersman had never before seemed so satisfied with his actions or displayed such dignity as he did in his magistrate's role.

9

THE FINAL YEARS

DANIEL'S HAPPINESS was not to continue. A treaty signed on April 30, 1803, between the United States and France would have a great impact on his future. On March 9 of the following year Spain officially transferred Louisiana to France, and the next day France transferred it to the United States. President Jefferson had completed the Louisiana Purchase. The cost of the territory from which all or part of thirteen new states would be formed was fifteen million dollars, or approximately three cents per acre.

The United States did not immediately replace the Spanish government in Missouri. And when the American officials did arrive, they came with instructions from Jefferson to make as few changes as possible. Boone therefore continued as syndic for some time after the Louisiana Purchase. Even years after his commission had expired, people with civil disputes would come to the "Justice Tree," submit themselves to Boone's judgments, and consider them binding.

Of most immediate concern to the inhabitants of Missouri was whether or not the change in government would affect their ownership of land. The United States land commission did not reach Missouri until months after the purchase, and the volume of cases to be examined caused a lengthy backlog in the hearings. Testimony on Boone's claims was not taken until February 13, 1806. Daniel had not learned enough prudence from his Kentucky experiences. He had kept all the papers which verified his grants and there were no cross-filings on his claims, but he had also relied upon Delassus's word that as syndic he need not conform to the standard validation practices required by Spanish law. Therefore, he had not bothered to clear ten acres annually on each of his two tracts until one-tenth of the entire acreage had been improved, nor had he filed the necessary papers in New Orleans to obtain the Spanish governor's approval of a permanent title. Delassus had told him that it was customary to exempt officials from this lengthy process. But that was a Spanish, not an American, custom. Daniel had not even built his cabin on his own land. He had no way of demonstrating conclusive ownership of his property.

The commission's recommendation that Boone's "claim ought not to be confirmed" was not officially adopted until December 1, 1809. Daniel had known the verdict would be unfavorable for some time. But he now had influential friends in high places who were willing to try to right this injustice. Judge John Coburn, a former land commissioner, championed Boone's cause, and probably wrote the petition presented to Congress for the old pioneer. Another friend, Colonel Return Jonathan Meigs, the former commander of St. Charles County from 1804 to 1806, was now in the Eleventh Congress and on the Public Lands Committee. He returned a favorable report on Boone's petition and was equally determined to see that Boone received some benefit from his years of service to his country.

While waiting for action on his request to Congress for some compensation for his lands, Daniel led the normal life of a wilderness hunter. He had a few close escapes from the Osage Indians, but the old trapper had forgotten none of the tricks that had enabled him to keep his scalp for three-quarters of a century. After an absence of ten years Daniel also had mellowed in his feelings about Kentucky. Sometime about 1810 he was in Kentucky making his way to the Indiana shore of the Ohio River to visit with his brother Squire when the now-famous meeting took place between Boone and John James Audubon. The ornithologist was then in his mid-twenties and had already begun to capture the beauty of America's birds in his drawings. Boone took an immediate liking to his new companion. Audubon reciprocated the feeling and set down the following example of premier marksmanship on the part of his new seventy-six-year-old friend:

Barking off squirrels is delightful sport, and in my opinion requires a greater degree of accuracy than any other. I first witnessed this manner of procurring squirrels whilst near the town of Frankfort. The performer was the celebrated Daniel Boon. We walked out together, and followed the rocky margins of the Kentucky River until we reached a piece of flat land thickly covered with black walnuts, oaks and hickories. As the general mast was a good one that year, squirrels were seen gambolling on every tree around us. My companion, a stout, hale, and athletic man, dressed in a homespun huntingshirt, bare-legged and moccasined, carried a long and heavy rifle, which, as he was loading it, he said had proved efficient in all his former undertakings, and which he hoped would not fail on this occasion, as he felt proud to show me his skill. The gun was wiped, the powder measured, the ball patched with a six-hundred-thread linen, and the charge sent home with a hickory rod. We moved not a step from the place, for the squirrels were so numerous that it was unnecessary to go after them. Boon pointed to one of these animals which had observed us, and was crouched on a branch about fifty paces distant, and bade me mark well the spot where the ball should hit. He raised his piece gradually, until the *bead* (that being the name given by the Kentuckians to the *sight*) of the barrel was brought to a line with the spot which he intended to hit. The whip-like report resounded through the woods and along the hills in repeated echoes. Judge of my surprise, when I perceived that the ball had hit the piece of bark immediately beneath the squirrel, and shivered it into splinters, the concussion produced by which had killed the animal and sent it whirling through the air, as if it had been blown up by the explosion of a powder magazine. Boon kept up his firing, and before many hours had elapsed, we had procured as many squirrels as we wished; for you must know, that to load a rifle requires only a moment, and that if it is wiped once after each shot, it will do duty for hours. Since that first interview with our veteran Boon, I have seen many other individuals perform the same feat.

Audubon also recounted a tale which Boone had told him during the night they spent together. He stated that Boone "related to me the following account of his powers of memory, which I lay before you, kind reader, in his own words, hoping that the simplicity of his style may prove interesting to you." The reader must exercise some caution in accepting "Boone's" account told "in his own words." It is an ironic truism of the Boone biographies that the narratives taken from Boone's "own mouth" seem to have received the most "improvement." Audubon, like Filson, probably kept the core of Boone's story but polished the rhetoric of the pioneer a bit too obviously.

"I was once," said he, "on a hunting expedition on the banks of the Green River, when the lower parts of this State (Kentucky) were still in the hands of nature, and none but the sons of the soil were looked upon as its lawful proprietors. We Virginians had for some time been waging a war of intrusion upon them, and I, amongst the rest, rambled through the woods in pursuit of their race, as I now would follow the tracks of any ravenous animal. The Indians outwitted me one dark night, and I was as unexpectedly as suddenly made a prisoner by them. The trick had been managed with great skill; for no sooner had I extinguished the fire of my camp, and laid me down to rest, in full security, as I thought, than I felt myself seized by an indistinguishable number of hands, and was immediately pinioned, as if about to be led to the scaffold for execution. To have attempted to be refractory, would have proved useless and dangerous to my life; and I suffered myself to be removed from my camp to theirs, a few miles distant, without uttering even a word of complaint. You are aware, I dare say, that to act in this manner was the best policy, as you understand that by so doing, I proved to the Indians at once, that I was born and bred as fearless of death as any of themselves.

"When we reached the camp, great rejoicings were exhibited. Two squaws and a few papooses appeared particularly delighted at the sight of me, and I was assured, by very unequivocal gestures and words, that on the morrow, the mortal enemy of the Red-skins would cease to live. I never opened my lips, but was busy contriving some scheme which might enable me to give the rascals the slip before dawn. The women immediately fell a searching about my hunting-shirt for whatever they might think valuable, and, fortunately for me, soon found my flask filled with *monongahela* (that is, reader, strong whisky). A terrible grin was exhibited on their murderous countenances, while my heart throbbed with joy at the anticipation of their intoxication. The crew immediately began to beat their bellies and sing, as they passed the bottle from mouth to mouth. How often did I wish the flask ten times its size, and filled with aqua-fortis! I observed that the squaws drank more freely than the warriors, and again my spirits were about to be depressed, when the report of a gun was heard at a distance. The Indians all jumped on their feet. The singing and drinking were both brought to a stand, and I saw, with inexpressible joy, the men walk off to some distance and talk to the squaws. I knew that they were consulting about me, and I foresaw that in a few moments the warriors would go to discover the cause of the gun having been fired so near their camp. I expected that the squaws would be left to guard me. Well, Sir, it was just so. They returned; the men took up their guns, and walked away. The squaws sat down again, and in less than five minutes had my bottle up to their dirty mouths, gurgling down their throats the remains of the whisky.

"With what pleasure did I see them becoming more and more drunk, until the liquor took such hold of them that it was quite impossible for these women to be of any service. They tumbled down, rolled about, and began to snore: when I, having no other chance of freeing myself from the cords that fastened me, rolled over and over towards the fire, and, after a short time, burned them asunder. I rose to my feet, stretched my stiffened sinews, snatched up my rifle, and, for once in my life, spared that of Indians. I now recollect how desirous I once or twice felt to lay open the skulls of the wretches with my tomahawk; but when I again thought upon killing beings unprepared and unable to defend themselves, it looked like murder without need, and I gave up the idea.

"But, Sir, I felt determined to mark the spot, and walking to a thrifty ash sapling, I cut out of it three large chips, and ran off. I soon reached the river, soon crossed it, and threw myself deep into the cane-brakes, imitating the tracks of an Indian with my feet, so that no chance might be left for those from whom I had escaped to overtake me.

"It is now nearly twenty years since this happened, and more than five since I left the Whites' settlements, which I might probably never have visited again, had I not been called on as a witness in a lawsuit that was pending in Kentucky, and which I really believe would never have been settled, had I not come forward, and established the beginning of a certain boundary line. This is the story, Sir.

"Mr ———— moved from Old Virginia into Kentucky, and having a large tract granted to him in the new State, laid claim to a certain parcel of land adjoining Green River, and as chance would have it, took for one of his corners the very Ash tree on which I had made my mark, and finished his survey of some thousands of acres, beginning, as it is expressed in the deed, 'at an Ash marked by three distinct notches of the tomahawk of a white man.'

"The tree had grown much, and the bark had covered the marks; but somehow or other, Mr ———— heard from someone all that I have already said to you, and thinking that I might remember the spot alluded to in the deed, but which was no longer discoverable, wrote for me to come and try at least to find the place or the tree. His letter mentioned that all my expenses should be paid, and not caring much about . . . going back to Kentucky, I started and met Mr ————. After some conversation, the affair with the Indians came to my recollection. I considered for a while, and began to think that after all I could find the very spot, as well as the tree, if it was yet standing.

"Mr ———— and I mounted our horses, and off we went to the Green River Bottoms. After some difficulties, for you must be aware, Sir, that great changes have taken place in those woods, I found at last the spot where I had crossed the river, and waiting for the moon to rise, made for the course in which I thought the Ash tree grew. On approaching the place, I felt as if the Indians were there still, and as if I was still a prisoner among them. Mr ———— and I camped near what I conceived the spot, and waited until the return of day.

"At the rising of the sun, I was on foot, and after a good deal of musing, thought that an Ash tree then in sight must be the very one on which I had made my mark. I felt as if there could be no doubt of it, and mentioned my thought to Mr ————. 'Well, Colonel Boon,' said he, 'if you think so, I hope it may prove true, but we must have some witnesses; do you stay here about, and I will go and bring some of the settlers whom I know.' I agreed. Mr ———— trotted off, and I, to pass the time, rambled about to see if a deer was still living in the land. But ah! Sir, what a wonderful difference thirty years makes in the country! Why, at the time when I was caught by the Indians, you would not have walked out in any direction for more than a mile without shooting a buck or a bear. There were then thousands of buffaloes on the hills in Kentucky; the land looked as if it never would become poor; and to hunt in those days was a pleasure indeed. But when I was left to myself on the banks of the Green

River, I dare say for the last time in my life, a few *signs* only of deer were to be seen, and, as to a deer itself, I saw none.

"Mr _____ returned, accompanied by three gentlemen. They looked upon me as if I had been WASHINGTON himself, and walked to the Ash tree, which I now called my own, as if in quest of a long lost treasure. I took an axe from one of them, and cut a few chips off the bark. Still no signs were to be seen. So I cut again until I thought it was time to be cautious, and I scraped and worked away with my butcher knife, until I *did* come to where my tomahawk had left an impression in the wood. We now went regularly to work, and scraped at the tree with care, until three hacks as plain as any three notches ever were, could be seen. Mr _____ and the other gentlemen were astonished, and, I must allow, I was as much surprised as pleased myself. I made affidavit of this remarkable occurrence in presence of these gentlemen. Mr _____ gained his cause. I left Green River for ever and came to where we now are; and, Sir, I wish you a good night."

In a somewhat similar story, Boone was said to have settled a land dispute by stating that the certain tree upon which the case hinged was one in which he had hidden an empty whiskey bottle. Some chopping and scraping at the tree in question soon revealed the bottle, now encased in wood. It should also be noted that the first part of Boone's composite tale documented a fourth, and previously unrecorded, Indian captivity.

By 1811, the British were inspiring Indian attacks upon Missouri. When Daniel Boone learned of the formal declaration of war in 1812, he was among the first volunteers for the army. He was indignant when he was refused enlistment because he was too old for combat; he was only seventy-eight. Daniel was not actively engaged in the fighting, but served when and where he could, as a sentry and frontier doctor.

For Boone, 1813 was a bad year. Rebecca, his uncomplaining wife for fifty-six years, died on March 18 at the age of seventy-four. Soon exaggerated estimates of the size of an attacking Indian force reached the ears of Flanders Callaway and made him decide to abandon his farm. Sometime in 1813 or 1814 he loaded Boone's manuscript autobiography into his canoe along with other goods, but the vessel struck a snag and overturned. The only sustained description of the frontiersman's life that really was in his "own words" was lost forever. At Daniel's age, dictation proved such a tedious chore that he gave up the idea of reconstructing the work for a time.

Almost as if to rub salt in this wound, the book-length poem *The Mountain Muse*, written by his wife's nephew Daniel Bryan, was published in 1813. It was Bryan's attempt to produce an American epic based on Boone's life and adventures and was intended to be similar in scope to Milton's *Paradise Lost*. Poetically, it was a disaster. Daniel sincerely regretted that Bryan was a relative, for he felt that he "could not sue him for slander." In the understated irony typical of his dry humor, he added that such works "ought to be left until the person was put in the ground."

If Daniel thought that no further problems could possibly occur in this one year, he was deluding himself. On the day before Christmas, the Congressional Committee on Public Lands brought in another report favorable to substantiating Boone's 10,000-arpent claim, but for some unknown reason the nonvoting delegate from the Missouri Territory stated that he knew Boone desired only his original grant of 1,000 arpents. Assuming that the representative expressed Daniel's wishes, the sponsors changed the act accordingly. When Boone learned the provisions of the special bill, signed by President Madison on February 10, 1814, he was furious. He said that he was no beggar and no pauper, and he threatened to write a letter to the Speaker of the House refusing the gift. But Congress was not in session. Daniel's family eventually persuaded him to keep the land.

He had to sell the entire tract in May 1815 to appease the creditors from Kentucky who had read of the government grant and hurried to Missouri to collect their debts. The last man to present a claim against Daniel Boone was the husband of an orphan girl, perhaps Chloe Flinn, who had received a gift of land from the generous old pioneer. It now turned out that someone had a previous or better claim to the land. The husband demanded compensation and refused to stop badgering Boone even when he was told that there was no money left. According to Nathan Boone, his father, "vexed at the greedy, unfeeling disposition the fellow manifested, finally told him in a quiet way, that he thought he had come a great distance to suck a bull, & he reckoned he would have to go home dry."

Daniel traveled a good deal for a man his age, both before and after the War of 1812. He reached Kansas and perhaps even Yellowstone, for he intended to explore the Rocky Mountains. Reports indicated that he was much interested in seeing California as well. Officers at Fort Osage near the site of the present Kansas City reported that Boone spent two weeks with them sometime in 1816 before leaving "for the River Platt, some distance above." The Platte River would have formed a likely route for an explorer on his way to the Yellowstone country.

Even if Daniel did not reach all of these places, his dreams lived on and motivated his descendants. His son Daniel Morgan Boone is reported to have been one of the first settlers of Kansas in 1827. His grandson Albert Gallatin Boone explored the Rocky Mountains, was prominent in negotiations of Indian treaties with the western tribes, and was an early settler of Colorado. Kit Carson, Fremont's famous scout on his transcontinental trek, was also a distant relation of Daniel's and coincidentally was appointed, along with Albert Gallatin Boone, by President Grant to negotiate the Indian treaty which ceded San Juan County, Colorado, to the United States.

In 1816, Daniel made a trip to the house of Dr. John Jones, the husband of one of his granddaughters. He had a double purpose, medical treatment for scrofula and a final attempt at dictating the story of his life, at least up to his migration to Missouri. This second narrative was never completed and the manuscript was lost after Dr. Jones's sudden death about the year 1842. Daniel never did have his say.

A letter from this period has survived, however. It tends to verify that in later years Boone thought a good deal about religion, even if he never formally joined a particular church.

october the 19th 1816

Deer Sister

    With pleasuer I Rcd a Later from your sun Samuel Boone who
informs me that you are yett Liveing and in good health Consid-
ing your age I wright to you to Latt you know I have Not forgot you
and to inform you of my own Situation Sence the Death of your
Sister Rabacah I leve with flanders Calaway But am at present at my
sun Nathans and in tolarabel halth you Can gass at my feilings by
your own as we are So Near one age I Need Not write you of our
satuation as Samuel Bradley or James grimes Can inform you of
Every Surcomstance Relating to our famaly and how we Leve in this
World and what Chance we Shall have in the next we know Not for
my part I am as ignerant as a Child all the Relegan I have to Love and
fear god beleve in Jeses Christ Don all the good to my Nighbour and
my self that I Can and Do as Little harm as I Can help and trust on
gods marcy for the Rest and I beleve god neve made a man of my
prisepel to be Lost and I flater my Self Deer sister that you are well
on your way in Cristianaty gave my Love to all your Childran and all
my frends fearwell my Deer sister

                                 Daniel Boone

Mrs. Sarah Boone
NB I Rcd a Later yesterday from sister Hanah peninton by hir
grand sun Dal Ringe She and all hir Childran are Well at present
                                       DB

One account stated that 1816 was also the year of Daniel
Boone's last hunt. Nathan, however, said that his father went
hunting with James Boone, his grandson, in the winter of
1817. On the latter trip, Daniel seemed to gain strength when
once again in his beloved wilderness. But after a few days he
felt the numbing effects of the elements. He was too cold to go
on and remained at this granddaughter Van Bibber's cabin at
Loutre Lick, where he became seriously ill. Nathan was sent
word of his condition, assumed the worst, and ordered a coffin
to be made. He was a bit premature. Arriving at the Van Bibber home, he found that Daniel had been treated by a passing
doctor and was well on the way to recovery. When Boone saw
the coffin his son had had made for him, he said it was too
rough and uncouth, and proceeded to have a better one

fashioned out of cherry according to his directions. The first coffin was used to bury a relative. The second one, much to the fright of the small grandchildren, was stored in the cabin loft by Daniel until it was needed.

By summer, Boone was strong enough to make another journey to Kentucky. It was probably on this trip, or perhaps the earlier one on which he met Audubon, that Boone finally paid off his remaining creditors. It had taken more than thirty years, but at last the stigma of debt was removed. He had no records or accounts; he paid whatever each man said was due him. Tradition has it that when Daniel returned to his home in Missouri he had fifty cents left in his pocket.

Chester Harding, an American portrait painter of some note, made a trip from St. Louis in June 1820 to capture the old pioneer's likeness on canvas. Harding, the best teller of the tale, noted that Boone was a hard man to find and not well known by his neighbors. The statement was a bit farfetched, but it added interest to the story.

I found that the nearer I got to his dwelling, the less was known of him. When within two miles of his house, I asked a man to tell me where Colonel Boone lived. He said he did not know any such man. "Why, yes, you do," said his wife. "It is that white-headed old man who lives on the bottom, near the river." A good illustration of the proverb, that a prophet is not without honor save in his own country.

I found the object of my search engaged in cooking his dinner. He was lying in his bunk, near the fire, and had a long strip of venison wound around his ramrod, and was busy turning it before a brisk blaze, and using salt and pepper to season his meat. I at once told him the object of my visit. I found that he hardly knew what I meant. I explained the matter to him and he agreed to sit. He was ninety years old, and rather infirm; his memory of passing events was much impaired, yet he would amuse me every day by his anecdotes of his earlier life. I asked him one day, just after his description of one of his long hunts, if he never got lost, having no compass. "No," he said, "I can't say as ever I was lost, but I was *bewildered* once for three days."

Daniel's humor was dry to the last.

The end came a few months later. Daniel had been taken

130

ill at the home of Flanders Callaway, but feeling his condition had improved he attempted to ride back to Nathan's home. The sickness recurred, supposedly brought on by an overindulgence of sweet potatoes. He was again attended by Dr. Jones, but refused medication. Daniel said that this was the last time he would be sick and he was not afraid to die. He expired three days later, just before sunrise on September 26, 1820.

Even beyond the grave it seemed that Daniel Boone could not control his "itching foot." There was still another journey for Daniel and Rebecca to make. After a strong appeal by the Kentucky legislature in 1845, the people of Missouri agreed to have the remains of the Boones moved to Frankfort where they would be reinterred and provided, it was promised, with a fitting monument. There were speeches, a full-dress military parade, a salute with rifles and swords, and taps—almost all the earmarks of the civilized life which Daniel had tried so hard to avoid. No irony was intended, of course, only the greatest honor. Still, one must wonder what the pioneer really would have thought of all this pomp. And might not a knowing half-smile have crossed his face when in 1880 the Kentucky politicians finally got around to erecting the promised monument, only thirty-five years late?

Epilogue

A STUDY OF THE LIFE of Daniel Boone would not be complete without some consideration of his emblematic or spiritual contributions to the westward expansion of America. The physical contributions—the trails blazed, the Indians fought, the forts and communities established—have already been documented. Yet there are wider implications in the benefits to exploration and settlement of his actual deeds. From his "discovery" of Kentucky in 1769 in his thirty-fifth year until decades past his death in 1820, through manifold political and socioeconomic changes in America, Boone remained a valuable constant. He epitomized the American way of life, the patterns which the Revolutionary War was fought to preserve. Nationally Boone was, and perhaps still is, the embodiment of the representative man, the ideal of frontier independence and virtue. In a country whose history has been dominated by continuing migration, the majority of early Americans believed themselves to be pioneers to some extent and, as such, identified with Boone as their hero.

In much the same way Boone also mirrored one very central American concern—the conflict of civilization and the wilderness. Which was the ideal state? On the one hand Boone was the pioneer, a man happy to do his part to help civilize the frontier and to praise these improvements. But on the other hand, as a hunter and man of nature, Boone was appalled at the encroachments of civilization and retreated before its corrupting influence to insure his own happiness. These contradictory impulses are still with us. Farms and forests, factories and parks, energy economics and ecology—all are pairs of opposites which are integral though unreconciled parts of the American self-image that Boone represented.

Boone as the "spirit of America" is an intangible that cannot be separated from the man and his endeavors. But his varied careers—explorer, adventurer, wagoner, husband, father, farmer, surveyor, land speculator, conservationist, hunter, military commander, spy, scout, sheriff, coroner, tavern proprietor, elected representative, and Spanish magistrate—were mere occupations, just so many categories which tell little of the essential unity of Daniel Boone. As a man equally pragmatic and romantic, his achievements and fame live on for Americans in this dual role of pioneer and preserver because—imagined, desired, or enacted—this is the dual role of the American people, as well.

Significantly, Boone still functions as an ideal or representative man, as a model worthy of emulation. It is not widely known, but Dan Beard, the founder of the Boy Scouts of America, a group that has turned and is turning millions of young Americans into trailblazers and woodsmen, stated that he based his conception of this organization upon the following premise: "A society of scouts to be identified with the greatest of all Scouts, Daniel Boone, and to be known as the Sons of Daniel Boone."

Bibliographic Note

THE PRIMARY AND SECONDARY materials pertinent to the life of Daniel Boone are so voluminous that even a partial listing would swell this volume far beyond its present size. In this selected bibliography, therefore, I make no attempt to be comprehensive. I refer the reader to William Harvey Miner's *Daniel Boone: Contributions Toward a Bibliography of Writings concerning Daniel Boone* (1901; rpt. New York, 1970) for pre-1900 references, and to the bibliography in Willard Rouse Jillson's *The Boone Narrative* (Louisville, Ky., 1932). More recent bibliographies that concentrate on works concerning Boone published before the Civil War can be found in Richard Slotkin's "Emergence of a Myth: John Filson's 'Daniel Boone Narrative' and the Literature of the Indian Wars, 1638–1848" (Ph.D. dissertation, Brown University, 1967); and Michael A. Lofaro's "The Genesis of the Biographical Image of Daniel Boone" (Ph.D. dissertation, University of Maryland, 1975). The card catalogs of almost all large libraries and other usual bibliographic sources will yield a generous list of post-1930 works on the pioneer.

Although a number of general works dealing with the Kentucky frontier are mentioned in this book, the interested reader is again directed to more detailed surveys of available literature. J. Winston Coleman's *A Bibliography of Kentucky History* (Lexington, Ky., 1949), Willard Rouse Jillson's *Books on Kentucky Books and Writers: A Bibliography [1784–1950]* (Frankfort, Ky., 1951), and Jacqueline Bull's annual compilation of "Writings on Kentucky History" for the years 1948 through 1962, which was published irregularly in *The Register of the Kentucky Historical Society*, with the last list appearing in April 1968, should all prove useful in this regard. A separate imprint was also issued by the Kentucky Historical Society for the earlier bibliographies: *Writings on Kentucky History, 1948–1955* (Frankfort, Ky., n.d.), compiled by Jacqueline Bull and Frances L. S. Dugan.

After nearly 200 years, during which numerous biographies of Daniel Boone have appeared, it would be folly to pretend that the majority of events and episodes here recounted are startlingly new. But a biographer, consciously or unconsciously, creates and projects a particular image of his subject through the selection of data. In an effort to maintain the closest possible ties with primary source material, I have drawn heavily upon the large Draper Manuscript Collection of the State Historical Society of Wisconsin. Credit for most of the new material presented in this study, therefore, belongs to Dr. Lyman Copeland Draper, the superb nineteenth-century investigative historian of the trans-Appalachian West.

The results of Draper's more than fifty years of gathering and arranging manuscript materials fill 486 volumes, which are now divided into fifty series, each with its own alphabetical designation. His five-volume "Life of Boone," which covers the frontiersman's life through 1778, is the acknowledged authoritative work on the subject. My present project of an edition of the "Life" runs well over 800 pages in typescript. Draper unfortunately never completed his book, but did leave approximately forty additional volumes of manuscripts and notes which related directly to Boone's career and which can be used to reconstruct the story of the second half of the pioneer's life. The most frequently consulted of the fifty series of the Draper volumes were the following:

B   Draper's "Life of Boone" (5 vols.)

C   Boone MSS. (32 vols.)

S   Draper's Notes (33 vols. Volume 6S contains Draper's 1851 interviews in Missouri with a number of Boone's relatives. The large section dealing with the information given by Nathan Boone and his wife is quite important.)

CC   Kentucky MSS. (30 vols.)

There is also a good deal of material in series J, the George

Rogers Clark MSS. (65 vols.), and in series QQ, the Preston Papers (6 vols.), as well as a number of items scattered throughout the collection.

The best biography of Boone published to date is unquestionably John Bakeless's *Daniel Boone: Master of the Wilderness* (1939; rpt. Harrisburg, Pa., 1965). Bakeless was the first biographer to make full use of the Draper Manuscript Collection. His work is especially valuable for the post-1778 period because of its adept organization of far-ranging source materials.

Other biographies of particular interest include: John Filson's *The Discovery, Settlement And present State of Kentucke: . . . To which is added . . . I. The Adventures of Col. Daniel Boon . . .* (Wilmington, Del., 1784), the first "autobiography"; John Trumbull's very popular condensed edition of Filson's work, *The Adventures of Colonel Daniel Boon . . .* (Norwich, Conn., 1786); C. Wilder's printing of the *Life and Adventures of Colonel Daniel Boon . . .* (1823; rpt. New York, 1916), which added a "Continuation of the Life of Colonel Boon" to the Trumbull text; Timothy Flint's *Biographical Memoir of Daniel Boone* (1833; rpt. New Haven, Conn., 1967) (a runaway best-seller of its day partly because of a number of romantic fabrications, but one that cannot be dismissed out of hand because of Flint's interviews with Boone); John Mason Peck's *Life of Daniel Boone, the Pioneer of Kentucky*, in *The Library of American Biography*, 2d series, vol. 13, ed. Jared Sparks (Boston, 1847) (a minister's idealized view of the frontiersman, but again one based upon personal interviews); and Reuben Gold Thwaites's *Daniel Boone* (New York, 1902), a work drawn in part from the Draper Manuscripts. This list is far from complete. Daniel Boone has been and still is a figure that stirs the interest of innumerable biographers.

The magnificent amount of available source material is due in large measure to the diligence of the local historians of Kentucky. Two journals, *The Register of the Kentucky Historical Society* and *The Filson Club Historical Quarterly*, amply repay even the most casual perusal. The many volumes published by the Filson Club from 1884 to the present provide a large additional fund of information. Other valuable collections include: the material on Boone in the *Missouri Historical Review* (especially the articles on Boone's life in Missouri by William S. Bryan); the *Mississippi Valley Historical Review*, which is now *The Journal of American History; American Archives; American State Papers; Calendar of Virginia State Papers; The State Records of North Carolina; Pennsylvania Archives;* and the *Pennsylvania Magazine of History and Biography.*

Other selected works of interest relating directly or indirectly to the life of Daniel Boone include:

Abbott, John S. C. *Daniel Boone, Pioneer of Kentucky.* New York, 1872.

Alvord, Clarence W. "Daniel Boone." *American Mercury* 8 (June 1926): 266–70.

————. *The Mississippi Valley in British Politics.* 2 vols. Cleveland, Ohio, 1917.

Audubon, John James. *Delineations of American Scenery and Character,* ed. Francis H. Herrick. New York, 1926.

————. *Ornithological Biography.* 5 vols. Edinburgh, 1831–1839.

Audubon, Maria R. *Audubon and His Journals.* 2 vols. 1897; rpt. New York, 1972.

Bancroft, George. *The History of the United States from the Discovery of the American Continent.* 10 vols. Boston, 1834–1874.

Beard, Dan. *Hardly a Man Is Now Alive: The Autobiography of Dan Beard.* New York, 1939.

Bodley, Temple. *George Rogers Clark.* New York, 1926.

————. *History of Kentucky.* 4 vols. Chicago, 1928.

Bogart, William H. *Daniel Boone and the Hunters of Kentucky.* New York, 1857.

Bruce, Henry Addington. *Daniel Boone and the Wilderness Road.* New York, 1910.

Bryan, Daniel. *The Mountain Muse: Comprising the Adventures of Daniel Boone and the Powers of Virtuous and Refined Beauty.* Harrisonburg, Va., 1813.

Clark, Jerry E. *The Shawnee.* Lexington, Ky., 1977.

Clark, Thomas D. *Frontier America.* New York, 1959.

————. *A History of Kentucky.* New York, 1937.

————. *Kentucky, Land of Contrast.* New York, 1968.

————. *Simon Kenton, Kentucky Scout*. New York, 1943.

De Voto, Bernard, ed. *The Journals of Lewis and Clark*. Boston, 1953.

Durrett, Reuben T. *Bryant's Station*. Louisville, Ky., 1897.

————. *John Filson, The First Historian of Kentucky*. Louisville, Ky., 1884.

————. Manuscript Collection. Joseph Regenstein Library, University of Chicago.

Elliott, Lawrence. *The Long Hunter: A New Life of Daniel Boone*. New York, 1976.

Flint, Timothy. *Indian Wars of the West*. Cincinnati, Ohio, 1833.

French, Benjamin Franklin. *Biographia Americana; or a Historical and Critical Account of the Lives, Actions, and Writings of the Most Distinguished Persons in North America*. . . . New York, 1825.

Hall, James. *Legends of the West*. Philadelphia, 1832.

————. *Sketches of History, Life, and Manners in the West*. [Only volume 1 issued.] Cincinnati, Ohio, 1834.

Harding, Chester. *My Egotistigraphy*. Cambridge, Mass., 1866.

Henderson, Archibald. *The Transylvania Company and the Founding of Henderson, Ky*. Henderson, Ky., 1929.

Herrick, Francis Hobart. *Audubon the Naturalist: A History of His Life and Time*. 1917; rpt. New York, 1968.

Imlay, Gilbert. *A Topographical Description of the Western Territory of North America*. . . . London, 1793; Dublin, 1793; New York, 1793; London, 1797.

Jillson, Willard Rouse. *The Boone Narrative*. Louisville, Ky., 1932.

————. *Filson's Kentucke*. Louisville, Ky., 1930.

————. *The Kentucky Land Grants*. Louisville, Ky., 1925.

————. *Old Kentucky Entries and Deeds*. Louisville, Ky., 1926.

————. *Pioneer Kentucky*. Frankfort, Ky., 1934.

————. *Tales of the Dark and Bloody Ground*. Louisville, Ky., 1930.

Kellogg, Louise P., ed. *Frontier Advance on the Upper Ohio, 1778–1779*. Madison, Wis., 1916.

————, ed. *Frontier Retreat on the Upper Ohio, 1779–1781*. Madison, Wis., 1917.

Kenton, Edna. *Simon Kenton: His Life and Period, 1755–1836*. Garden City, N.Y., 1930.

Lester, William S. *The Transylvania Company*. Spencer, Ind., 1935.

Lewis, Virgil A. *History of the Battle of Point Pleasant*. Charleston, W.Va., 1909.

Marshall, Humphrey. *The History of Kentucky*. Frankfort, Ky., 1812.

McClung, John A. *Sketches of Western Adventure: Containing an Account of the Most Interesting Incidents Connected with the Settlement of the West*. Maysville, Ky., 1832.

Metcalf, Samuel L. *A Collection of Some of the Most Interesting Narratives of Indian Warfare in the West*. Lexington, Ky., 1821.

Moore, Arthur K. *The Frontier Mind: A Cultural Analysis of the Kentucky Frontiersman*. Lexington, Ky., 1957.

Ranck, George W. *Boonesborough: Its Founding, Pioneer Struggles, Indian Experiences, Transylvania Days, and Revolutionary Annals*. Louisville, Ky., 1901.

Rice, Otis K. *Frontier Kentucky*. Lexington, Ky., 1975.

Simms, William Gilmore. "Daniel Boone—The First Hunter of Kentucky." *Southern and Western Magazine* 1 (April 1845): 225–42.

Slotkin, Richard. *Regeneration through Violence: The Mythology of the American Frontier, 1600–1860*. Middletown, Conn., 1973.

Smith, Henry Nash. *Virgin Land: The American West as Symbol and Myth*. 1950; rpt. Cambridge, Mass., 1970.

Speed, Thomas. *The Wilderness Road*. Louisville, Ky., 1886.

Spraker, Hazel A. *The Boone Family*. Rutland, Vt., 1922.

Stoudt, John Joseph. "Daniel and Squire Boone—A Study in Historical Symbolism." *Pennsylvania History* 3 (1936): 27–40.

Thatcher, Benjamin Bussey. *Tales of the Indians, Being Prominent Passages of the History of the North American Natives*. Boston, 1831.

Thwaites, Reuben G., and Kellogg, Louise P., eds. *Documentary History of Dunmore's War, 1774*. Madison, Wis., 1905.

———. *Frontier Defense on the Upper Ohio, 1777–1778*. Madison, Wis., 1912.

———. *The Revolution on the Upper Ohio, 1775–1777*. Madison, Wis., 1908.

Turner, Frederick Jackson. *The Frontier in American History*. 1920; rpt. New York, 1962.

Van Noppen, John James, and Van Noppen, Ina Woestemeyer. *Daniel Boone, Backwoodsman: The Green Woods Were His Portion*. Boone, N.C., 1966.

Waller, George M. *The American Revolution in the West*. Chicago, 1976.

Walton, John. "Ghost Writer to Daniel Boone." *American Heritage* 6 (Oct. 1955): 10–13.

————. *John Filson of Kentucke*. Lexington, Ky., 1956.

Williams, William Carlos. *In the American Grain*. 1925; rpt. New York, 1956.

Wright, Louis B. *Culture on the Moving Frontier*. Bloomington, Ind., 1955.

Addenda

A number of works concerning Daniel Boone have appeared since the publication of the first edition of this book. Among these are:

Brown, William Dodd, ed. "The Capture of Daniel Boone's Saltmakers: Fresh Perspectives from Primary Sources." *The Register of the Kentucky Historical Society* 83 (1985): 1-19.

Lipton, Leah. *A Truthful Likeness: Chester Harding and His Portraits*. Washington, D.C., 1985: 42, 55-59.

————. "Chester Harding and the Life Portraits of Daniel Boone." *American Art Journal* 16 (1984): 4-19.

Lofaro, Michael A. "The Eighteenth Century 'Autobiographies' of Daniel Boone." *The Register of Kentucky Historical Society* 76 (1978): 85-97.

————. "From Boone to Crockett: The Beginnings of Frontier Humor." *Mississippi Folklore Register* 14 (1980): 57-74.

————. "Tracking Daniel Boone: The Changing Frontier in American Life." *The Register of the Kentucky Historical Society* 82 (1984): 321-33.

Although they do not necessarily focus directly on Daniel Boone, a number of articles by Neal O. Hammon provide invaluable data on early pioneer roads, trails, and surveys. Among these works are:

Hammon, Neal O. "Early Roads into Kentucky." *The Register of the Kentucky Historical Society* 68 (1970): 91-131.

————. "The First Trip to Boonesborough." *The Filson Club Historical Quarterly* 45 (1971): 249-63.

————. "Land Acquisition on the Kentucky Frontier." *The Register of the Kentucky Historical Society* 78 (1980): 297-321.

Index

Aix-la-Chapelle, Treaty of, 11
Allegheny Mountains, 22, 23-24
Allegheny River, 14
Appalachian Mountains, 11
Arbuckle, Captain Matthew, 71
Ashe County, N.C., 21
Asheton, Ralph, 2
Athens, Ky., 92
Attakullakulla (Leaning Wood), 44
Audubon, John James, meets
    Boone, 122-26
Augusta County, 42
Augusta, Mo., 117

Bakeless, John, 2
Bancroft, George, 13
Barrington, Lord, 23
Batts, Thomas, 10
Beard, Dan, 134
Beaver Creek, 24-25
Benton, Jesse, 54
Berks County, Pa., vii, 8
Big Bone Lick, 31
Big Jim (Shawnee), 38, 109
Big Lick, 41, 46
Big Sandy River, 22, 25, 115
Bird, Captain Henry, 95, 96
Blackfish (Shawnee), 66, 67, 79,
    89; adopts Boone, 75-76; attacks
    Boonesborough, 67, 83; cap-
    tures Boone, 72; death of, 91;
    negotiates with Boone, 80-83
Blackmore's Fort, 42
Blue Jacket (Shawnee), 110-11
Blue Licks, 40, 63, 70, 73, 79, 89,
    94, 105, 109-10, 113, 114; Battle

of, 103-105. *See also* Lower
    Blue Licks; Upper Blue Licks
Blue Ridge Mountains, 22, 26
Boiling Spring settlement, Ky., 49
Boone, Albert Gallatin (grandson),
    128
Boone, Daniel: adopted by Indi-
    ans, 75-76; ancestry of, 1-2; ap-
    pearance of, 14, 112, 122; auto-
    biography of, viii, ix, 111, 126-
    27, 128; in Battle of Blue Licks,
    102-105; birth of, vii, 3; at Boo-
    nesborough Convention, 49-50;
    brings family to Boonesbor-
    ough, 50; builds Fort Boone,
    47-48; captured, 27-29, 72-77,
    97, 123-24; compassion of, 20,
    32; court-martial of, 89-90;
    courtship and marriage of, 14-
    16; death of, vii, 129, 130-31;
    debts of, 25-26, 130; early years
    of, 3-9; education of, 4-5; explo-
    rations of, viii, 4, 19, 20-21, 22,
    23, 36-37, 128; fortifies Boones-
    borough, 78-79; humor of, 5-7,
    15, 16-17, 127, 128, 130; Indian
    names of, 25, 75, 76; land
    claims and disputes of, viii, 92,
    108, 111, 113-16, 117, 118-19,
    121, 127-28; military service of,
    17, 41, 42, 65, 89, 97, 112, 113;
    occupations of, 9, 12-14, 16,
    107-108, 109, 134; opens Wil-
    derness Road, 44-47; in political
    office, 63, 97, 111, 112, 117,
    119, 120; powers of memory of,

143

Callaway Flanders, 75, 78, 116, 126, 129, 131
Callaway, Jemima Boone. *See* Boone, Jemima
Callaway, Colonel Richard, 45, 49, 50, 60, 63, 79, 84-85; killed, 94-95; prefers charges against Boone, 89-90
Callaway, Mrs. Richard, 84, 88
Camel, Robert, 108
Campbell, Colonel Arthur, 53, 64
Camp Charlotte, Treaty of, 43, 54
Canada, 10, 24
Caperton, Captain Hugh, 113
Captain Johnny, 110
Captain Will, 27-28, 32
Carleton, Governor, 56
Carlisle, Pa., 8
Carson, Kit, 128
Carter, John, 45
Castle's-woods, Va., 37, 38
Charlottesville, Va., 97
Cherokees, 11, 16, 17, 21, 25, 36, 43-45, 50, 83; Treaty of Hard Labor with, 26; war parties of, 63
Chesapeake Bay, 56
Chillicothe, 76, 79, 96, 99, 105, 106
Chippewa, 92
Cincinnati, Ohio, 116
Clark, General George Rogers, 5, 39, 55, 64-65, 82, 96, 105, 109; and campaigns of 1778-1779, 91-92
Clark County, Ky., 116
Clendenin, Colonel William, 113
Clinch River, 26
Clinch Valley, 22, 37, 41
Coburn, Judge John, 121
Cocke, William, 48, 49
Coffee, Ambrose, 84
Collins, William, 85
Connolly, John, 56
Continental Congress, 51-52
Cooley, William (or Cool), 26-29
Coomes, William, 66

Cooper, James Fenimore, 63-64, 116
Cornstalk (Shawnee), 42-43, 54, 71, 73
Cornwallis, General Charles, 97-98
Cowan's Fort, 42
Crabtree, Isaac, 37-38
Crawford, Colonel William, 98
Croghan, George, 39
Cross-Creek, N.C. (Fayetteville), 44
Culpeper County, Va., 16
Culpeper, Va., 18
Cumberland Gap, 25, 26, 34, 35, 48
Cumberland Mountains, 13, 22
Cumberland River, 33, 36, 44, 66
Cumberland Valley, 8, 33
Cutbirth, Benjamin, 21-22, 36, 45

Daniel Boone's Palatinate, 117
Davie County, N.C., 9
De Beaujeu, 13-14
Declaration of Independence, 55, 64
Delassus, Carlos D., 116, 117, 118, 121
Delaware Indians, 42, 77
Delaware River, 11
De Peyster, Major, 95
De Quindre, Antoine Dagneaux, 81, 85
Detroit, 55, 71, 76, 80, 81, 82, 89, 91, 95, 97, 98
Dick's (Dix) River, 31, 49, 50
The Discovery, Settlement . . . of Kentucky, viii-ix, 111
Douglas, James, 39
Dragging Canoe (Cherokee), 44-45
Drake, Joseph, 33
Duncan, John, 42
Dunmore, Lord, 39, 40, 42, 51, 56, 76
Dutchman's Creek, N.C., 9
Dysart, James, 33

147

148

149

St. Charles County, Mo., vii, 115, 117, 121
St. Louis, Mo., 116, 118, 130
Stafford, William, 84
Station Camp Creek, 27
Staunton, Va., 97
Stone Mountain, 26
Stoner, Michael, 40-41, 45, 48
Stover, Jacob, 2
Strode's Station, 110
Stuart, John, 20, 26, 32; captured by Indians, 27-29; death of, 29-30
Sugar Tree Creek, 16, 18, 21, 24
Sycamore Shoals, 49; Treaty of, 44-45

Tahgahjute, 40. *See also* Logan
Tarleton, Colonel Banastre, 97
Tate, 19-20
Tate, Samuel, 46; son of, 46
Taylor, Hancock, 39
Tennessee, 17, 22
Todd, John, 65, 102, 103, 104
Todd, Major Levi, 101, 110
Trabue, Daniel, 69
Trade, Board of, 23
Translyvania, 65; founding of, 43-52; land rush into, 53; disputed claims in, 54-55. *See also* Richard Henderson; Transylvania Company
Transylvania Company, 43-45; claims Kentucky, 65.
Transylvania Convention, 49-50, 51
Treaty of Paris, 106
Trigg, Stephen, 102, 103
Trudeau, Don Zenon, 115, 116, 118
Turtle Creek Ravine, 13
Twitty, Captain William, 45-46
Twitty's Fort, 46

Upper Blue Licks, 30, 59, 61, 63, 96. *See also* Blue Licks; Lower Blue Licks

Van Bibber, 129
Vincennes, 91-92
Vinzant, Bery, 119
Virginia, 11, 24, 39, 43, 55-57, 56, 80, 81, 89, 90, 97
Virginia, Council of, 64, 66
Virginia Convention, 54-55, 64
Virginia legislature, 96-97

Wabash River, 109
Waddell, Colonel Hugh, 17
Walden's Creek (now Indian Creek), massacre at, 37-38
Walden's Ridge, 26
Walker, Felix, 45-47
War of 1812, 126, 128
War of Independence. *See* Revolutionary War
Warriors' Path, 13, 25, 26, 27, 29, 34, 45, 61, 66
Washington County, Tenn., 17
Washington, George, viii, 12, 14, 17, 39, 116, 126
Washington, Ky., 51
Watauga region, 36, 44, 58, 63
Watauga River, 44
Wayne, General Mad Anthony, 106, 114
Wea Indians, 92
Wilcoxen, George, 6
Wilderness Road, 29, 39, 44-47, 92, 114-15
Will, Captain, 72
Williams, Colonel, 55
Williamsburg, Va., 55, 64, 93
Winchester, Ky., 58
Winnebago Indians, 92
Wolf (Indian), 110
Woods, Francis, 119
Wyandots, 70, 98, 105

Xenia, Ohio, 77

Yadkin River, 9, 24-25
Yadkin Valley, 9, 17, 32, 35, 36, 37, 68
Yellow Creek, 40